THE POWER CENTRES

Driving Your Lifeforce Through The 7 Powers That Drive Your Life

RAJ GORSIA

Copyright © 2024 by Rajesh Gorsia

All rights reserved. No part of this publication may be reproduced, stored or transmitted in any form or by any means, electronic, mechanical, photocopying, recording, scanning, or otherwise without written permission from the publisher. It is illegal to copy this book, post it to a website, or distribute it by any other means without permission.

First Edition

ISBN: 9798322452416

Published By Rajesh Gorsia

www.withraj.com

Disclaimer:

The information presented in this book is based on the author's personal experiences and is intended for informational purposes only. It is not intended to be a substitute for professional medical or psychological advice, diagnosis, or treatment. Readers should seek the advice of qualified healthcare or mental health professionals for any medical or psychological concerns. The author and publisher disclaim any liability for the use or misuse of the information provided in this book.

Dedication

To all the students of life, the ones who never stop learning and exploring, this is for you.

To that lifeforce, I dedicate this to you. I am in service of you, I work through you.

To Dad, you keep reminding me how to stand up for myself and how to be a strong-hearted man who takes pride in everything he does, "either do it properly or don't do it at all." Your lessons have shaped me, and I'm forever grateful.

To Mum, you keep reminding me how to be such a wonderful caretaker of others, and how to take life less seriously by focusing on the little things that mean a lot.

Contents

Part One – Me

Introduction 2
My Journey 8
Pre-Flight Message 11

Part Two: The Power Centres

The Power Centre Pyramid 16
C1 - The Root Centre - The Power of The Ground 17
Wisdom 101 - The Power of Unifying Oneself 28
C2 - The Creative Centre — The Power of Being You 37
C3 - The Core Centre - The Power To Launch 48
The Lower Centres - The Power In Me 64
C4 - The Connection Centre — The Power of Me To We 67
C5 - The Expression Centre - The Power To Be A Roarer 87
C6 - The Vision Centre - The Power of The Lighthouse 104
C7 - The Crown Centre - The Power of Letting Go 128
Final Tool-Tips 144

Part Three - Beyond The Power Centres

The Power of The Path of Lifeforce 152
The Power of Spacial Awareness - The Left And Right Wings Of The Heart 158
The Power of The Duos - "As Above, So Below" 163
The Power of Power Stacking 173
The Third Force - The Power of Living In One Symmetry 177
Conclusion - The Power Of "Living Life" Unified 186
About the Author 196

Part One – Me

Here's what I've learnt and wish for you to learn.

This section provides some context, and instructions for how to get the most out of this book. So it isn't just another book, instead it's your book.

Introduction

"Now this is the story all about how, my life got flipped, turned upside-down, and I'd like to take a minute, just sit right there, I'll tell you how I became the prince of a town called Bel Air."
~ Will Smith

When I walked into my first office job at age 21, I felt this massive energy surge through my body. I had finally "made it". I was earning a salary of £23,000 a year, working in a beautiful location in the centre of London, and I was meeting my friends for drinks every Friday.

I felt like I was "rich" in levels of aliveness and enthusiasm. Well, that's what I felt some of the time, most of the time it felt like there was something in my way. The same aliveness that gave me excitement seemed to turn against me. Not just on Mondays, but every single day.

When I say aliveness, I mean energy. When I say turn against me, I mean my body and mind created feelings of danger and fight or flight. Not because a tiger had just approached me, but because of the mental idea that a tiger was forever following me.

The problem for someone who feels this way is that it feels like you cannot get rid of this tiger. I have learned that this tiger is a manifestation of the volcanic energy surging through the body.

Ever since I can remember, I have had a sensitive energy system. I dreaded shaking people's hands because I had sweaty palms and an overthinking mind. I dreaded being the centre of attention because my mind told me that it was dangerous.

Thank god I went on a journey to figure out what the hell was happening to me. Thank the voice in me for being curious enough to not give up. Thank life for having so many wondrous secrets that I never knew existed, and that many scientists can't even explain.

And finally, thank my deceased grandfather for naming me Rajesh.

Introduction

Raj means King. Rajesh means Lord of Kings. It can also be translated to "Leader of Leaders", which includes the Queens in the translation and better describes my duty.

My mum tells me that she wanted to name me something else, but my grandfather persisted and demanded that I be called Rajesh. Somehow he knew that I was meant to impact people in a powerful way.

You see, leader of leaders doesn't mean I am better than anyone or rule them. It means I am the trusted right hand man who shows the kings and queens of this world how to be the leaders of the kingdoms–the kingdoms of their inner and outer worlds. There is no hierarchy, there are only possibilities.

So that's who this book is for. For all of us humans who are trying to figure out how to lead and live our best life. "Leader" isn't a job title to me, it is a way of operating. It means being able to tap into that powerful force inside and unleash it.

* * *

An Invitation

This invitation is for you to drop everything you know so you can achieve a deeper knowing–a fresh knowing rather than a memory-based one. I often use the example of dating; if you've been hurt by your ex, it isn't fair to paint every single new person with the same paint as your ex. Unfortunately, we all (myself included) tend to do that through our habitual reactions. Let's do away with what we know because in the unknown there can be new discoveries, like landing in a new country and going exploring.

People often say to me that I am "so relaxed", but what they don't see is that there is a storm of stimulation occurring inside. That storm used to be my enemy but now I have learned to direct it toward the things that I was made to do.

That is the only way I was able to write this book. To drop all of the overthinking that comes with writing a book and instead focus on the insights and beauty that comes out of it. It's not really about me, it's about you, the reader.

Let's Start With How

In the next few chapters, I will introduce you to the topic of Power Centres, which are derived from the Chakras. I will also show you how they can reveal more of your abilities.

This book is my attempt at taking the wisdom from the ancient chakra system and redefining them as power centres.

The power centres are my way of representing the chakras in a clinical way—such that they are utilities, tools, and they have functional benefits that are clearly laid out. Rather than sounding like vague spiritual theories that require someone to be a full time yogi or follow certain kind of path to understand.

I am all for bridging the gap so that yogic science meets modern science, and the combination can be utilised in a practical way, for all kinds of people.

So you could say that the power centres are something else altogether—a fresh way of looking at things.

The word "power" awakens the chakras to a strong image for modern living—rather than the airy-fairy things that some people portray them as.

Having said that, I've maintained the sacredness of the chakras and yogic science in this book, as a foundation to the entire book. I've simply adapted it to make it more accessible.

* * *

You can think of these centres as parts of a whole system; a system of life's overall potential, acting as your driving forces and your teammates.

I will also talk about lifeforce (signified by Shakti), the prime power source of everything that's alive. This power source wants to move through the centres efficiently, lighting them up along the way.

Introduction

The lifeforce operates within us through these centres like an Amazon delivery journey. We want the flow to be fluid from centre to centre, all the way up to the final destination. But as you will discover in this book (or have already discovered), there are blocks that can get in the way.

This book could easily be seen as two, seven, or even ten separate books, because each centre, each polarity, and the teachings of lifeforce, liberation, action and unity can be books in themselves.

There are various schools of wisdom, both modern and ancient, western and eastern, scientific and spiritual which have endlessly talked of these topics in endless amounts of books.

Therefore, this book can either be a holistic foundation of various topics, or it can be read as a separate book per chapter.

It all depends on you and how you take this in. I have crafted the book to serve all purposes. It is an insight-focused book, not just informational, and it will send signals that you need to hear, if you listen very carefully.

Let's Continue With Why

So why did I choose the topic of human potential and decide to relate it to the ancient energy system as my first book? All will be revealed as you continue reading.

I am a British-born Indian, I rediscovered my roots after pretty much pushing away every Indian part of me for most of my life. As a part of that reconnection phase, my granddad spoke to me during meditation.

He helped me see that I am a living product of the fusion of ancient eastern wisdom and a modern western life; that my purpose is to channel the power to show others how they can operate in this way.

I have been practicing the science of energy and the science of personal mastery for over a decade. It may or may not sound like a long time, but I have been practicing intensely so it feels five times longer, like people who have a hobby of taking photos of planes.

They will spend their whole day outside of an airport, waiting and waiting, putting in the time and energy because they are thrilled by planes.

Then they do it over and over again, every day, no need for a day off, because it's energising rather than tiring to them.

That's me when it comes to practicing life mastery. Practicing, not studying. This isn't a theory, I am not a mindless robot that parrots theories from "successful researchers", or spiritual gurus.

You see, I understand the modern-day person who lives an everyday life, like me. I didn't have an enlightening experience in an ashram in India, my journey has been created over time through hard work, discipline and passion whilst living an everyday life, around everyday people, earning a living and seeking to live my best life.

All of the things that the ancient gurus and modern scientists talk about feel nice and warm on paper, but too many people message me wondering how they can experience it. They get the theory, but how do they practically relate it to their lives?

We are all looking for something, in some shape or form. I wish to see if I can help you make an operational shift that can move you towards what you want…

* * *

One thing I have learned is that bringing everything together, seeing how the cogs in the watch function together, and being able to use them in unison is what has allowed me to live life in the most enlightening way.

That's what I have always been good at, merging things together. Modern corporations will call this skill stacking. Skill stacking is when a skill such as creativity combines with strategy, or analytical skills combine with people leadership skills (basically my corporate career experience). They work better together rather than alone.

So I am going to present that to you in this book; a bunch of skills–a bunch of flavors that make a supreme recipe for life.

Also know that I am not perfect. I am human too. However, I wish to model the best that I know is possible and the best of me, with the aim of bringing the best part of you out.

Note:

After each chapter, I will place some questions for you to work on. Please don't skip these because they ensure that you are gaining the most value from the book. That way the book becomes your dance partner and your toolbox. Engagement is required.

You can spend as little as a one-minute mental note on these, or spend a whole day and notebook exercise contemplating. It's up to you. But please, just don't skip over them.

Here are your first questions.

✏ Questions to consider:

What would you love to explore through this book?

What's the story you've lived within your head?

What would you love to be your story from now on?

My Journey

"Let your mind start a journey through a strange new world. Leave all thoughts of the world you knew before. Let your soul take you where you long to be. Close your eyes, let your spirit start to soar, and you'll live as you've never lived before."
~ Erich Fromm

In 2011 I became interested in health and fitness, and in 2015 I began to practice yoga. I only joined a class because a pretty girl I fancied was going. I was not aware of it at the time, but it became a turning point in my life.

I began to feel tingling sensations in my forehead area and I asked the pretty yoga girl if she had felt this way before. She said no, so I figured it was some kind of headache.

But it continued to happen, and I came to the realisation that this wasn't a headache, it was more of a head pleasure. It felt like I was sitting on a vibrating chair that was altogether soothing and energising. Like a quiet storm of warm back rubs mixed with euphoric dancing.

This intrigue led me to start practicing yoga on my own (outside of the once-a-week class) and this is when I began to develop a regular and self-guided practice, which led me to learn more about the mind and the neurochemical process going on within me.

I began to feel calmer and more enthusiastic about life, but I was not aware that yoga was doing this for me. I just thought that my day was "going well". As an anxious person, "going well" is like a godsend. I wished and hoped for days when I felt a tiny bit different from my usual sweaty, nervous, tense and overthinking self.

For most of my life, I worried weeks in advance about a meeting or event, and simple things like having a conversation with someone about my weekend would be difficult.

My body was constantly overwhelmed and surging with energy at the same time, so weightlifting, running, or getting drunk were my greatest discoveries. They allowed me to feel a release from the body and mind disunity that I was experiencing.

I didn't know it back then, but these were just temporary relief processes versus transformational pathways. I no longer believe that exercise in itself alone is the solution to our inner challenges.

I ended up leaving work behind and traveling around the world on my own. I spent 20 months living unemployed and unrestricted.

I talk about the experience and my learnings on my YouTube page, but the summary would be that I came back with a fresh mode of thinking, and I was finally learning what it was like to be me. Me with fewer filters, me without pressure to be a certain way, just me.

I came back and went into maximum levels of intensity on meditation, yoga, kundalini practices, reading, health, and every angle that I could think of for developing myself. Course after course, podcast after podcast, practical session after practical session, and health refinement to the highest level.

It was an exponential change, like twenty years' worth of wisdom created in a short amount of time. Eventually, it was oozing out of my pores and I could not keep it to myself, so I decided that I must become a professional helper and guide to others.

Along my journey, I began to unlock life-changing wisdom about the human energy system. I learned how to direct the lifeforce energy to flow at the highest level by unblocking the flow centres (chakras), and the wisdom only keeps getting deeper as time passes by. There is no end to this evolution.

✏️ Questions to consider:

What does my story spark in you, related to your story?

Which parts can you relate to most?

What has been the main driver of your explorations in life so far? (i.e. what do you most value, enough to take action toward it)

What has been the main source of discouragement in your life so far? Try not to blame someone else, as tempting as it can be. Own the question.

Pre-Flight Message

"Chakras are organizational centres for the reception, assimilation, and transmission of lifeforce energy. They are the stepping stones between heaven and earth."
~ Anodea Judith

Before we take off, I want to be clear that everything I've written is based off of my personal experiences.

This book is a summation of my travails, with an aim to lead you towards yours.

Your Energy Has a System

The energy system of the chakras hasn't been taught at school because it's a system that most people do not understand.

It's difficult to teach this system to someone through logic. It can only be understood through awareness and practice, like playing the piano. These power centres hold the nature of life itself, so understanding them isn't always going to be easy, but it can be simple. For example, it's not always easy to get a joke, but when it clicks, it's awesome.

Skeptics may question the very existence of these power centres, to me that is like questioning whether bones exist.

The intellect seems to be great for things like Sudoku and math equations because math is a head game. But applying intellect to something that is way bigger than the head can belittle our experience of life. It's like saying love is just a release of chemicals. How dull would that be?

Even if it's true, it doesn't add value to my life. I'd rather feel love and experience it than logically having to know what it is.

From my experience, life can be fully experienced by letting go of the conclusions and predictions in my head.

Only then am I truly able to see life for what it is; I see the blank canvas, rather than trying to paint on top of art that I've predictably painted in my head.

Once I return back to the realisation that the intellect is a computing system that is trying to figure out life rather than actually knowing it, I am free. The machine is trying its best so it panics sometimes if it doesn't have answers. But if I let go of having all the answers, it eventually comes to me.

It's like a single cell in our body trying to disrupt the natural functioning of the entire body. It does it, and it creates the feeling that we call "stuck". The fluid isn't moving because the workers are hesitating, doubting, and getting blocked off by the powerful energy of our minds.

This is how physical and mental dis-ease seems to have worked for me. It's happened when one thought took over my body and my life and muddied it all. The singular one that forgets the whole one that it works with, like a soldier who attacks his own squad.

This is my way of introducing you to the power centre system and how blocks seemed to have occurred for me. I have moved past the blocks when I realised that this life is not about what my mind says, it is about my connection to everything as a whole.

* * *

These 7 power centres are like your best outfits. They are useful powers, like using fire to heat up food, and ice to cool down.

The purpose of this book is to present everything in an accessible way.

I take a strong stand for this work. It's moving through me, so I wish to clear the airy-fairy stuff so that Eastern wisdom is no longer just Eastern wisdom, but rather everyday human tools.

Tools that can pave the way towards commonly desirable traits such as "confidence", "strength", "freedom" and "connection".

That's definitely what it's done for me.

That's why I am reframing the chakras as power centres, to give them their well-deserved credibility as sources of power. Activating these powers can create limitless possibilities. Keep that in your awareness as you read.

In the next chapters, we will begin our journey and I will show you what I've learned. The point of your reading is to notice what sparks in you, what you'd like to learn more about, and to realise the shifts required for you to access the full expression of your existence.

If you are ready, let's begin the drive by going toward our first stop: the first power centre.

✏️ **Questions to consider:**

If you could expand by 5%, what would it be like?

What preconceived thoughts do you have about me and about this book?

What preconceived thoughts do you have about yourself?

What's wonderful about your mind?

Part Two: The Power Centres

This is the filler of the sandwich where I will go deeper into each centre. Only after writing and editing did I realise that the chapters get deeper as they continue.

This wasn't planned, but it also makes sense. The higher centres are less in form, lighter and subtler in their impact, so I have intuitively added more weight to those chapters.

These centres build on top of themselves; like having a strong foundation to a pyramid, with layers on top, beauty inside, and royalty resting deep within.

The Power Centre Pyramid

The diagram below illustrates the "7 powers that drive your life" mentioned in the subtitle. Take note of the dotted line running down the centre; that's the trajectory of lifeforce. Its boundless potential unfolds as it courses through each centre, merging them into a unified force, driving your existence forward with an electrifying momentum.

When these centres align into one cohesive unit, you unlock your utmost potential as a human being. It's akin to the unification of a vehicle, a skilled driver, and the drive to an extraordinary destination—all becoming one harmonious force, impelling you toward your ultimate purpose.

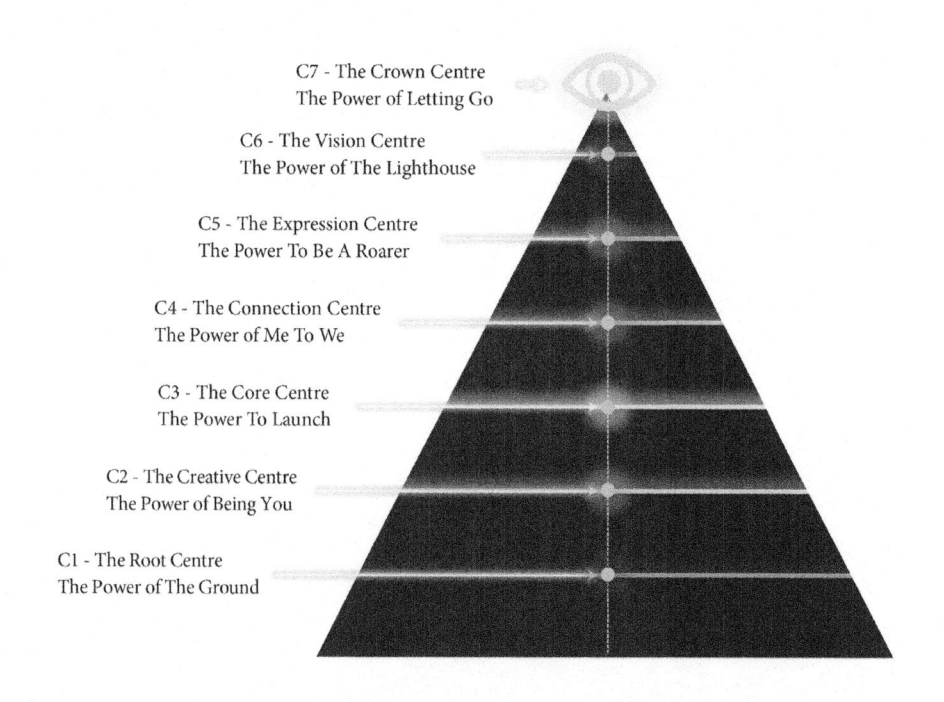

C7 - The Crown Centre
The Power of Letting Go

C6 - The Vision Centre
The Power of The Lighthouse

C5 - The Expression Centre
The Power To Be A Roarer

C4 - The Connection Centre
The Power of Me To We

C3 - The Core Centre
The Power To Launch

C2 - The Creative Centre
The Power of Being You

C1 - The Root Centre
The Power of The Ground

C1 - The Root Centre - The Power of The Ground

Chakra Name: *Muladhara*
Sanskrit Meaning: *Root Flow*
Location: *Base of the Spine*
Elemental Power: *Earth*

"A tree with strong roots laughs at storms."
~ Malay Proverb

We begin our journey at mother earth; the ground, the roots. Why? Because we are being pulled by gravity toward this earth only ever always. So logically it makes sense that we must have the same connection to the earth as a tree does. Rooted into it.

We all have a biological mother, but the true mother for everyone is the earth. You may laugh and say, "ah spiritual mumbo jumbo", but if you haven't noticed, I am quite a logical person, I like to make sense of things by putting the puzzle pieces together.

My entire career background has been in the field of IT and consultancy, and my upbringing has been playing computer games and getting excited about the tech specifications of devices. Ask my dad, he's a handyman, good with cars and engineering, while I spent most of my childhood indoors in my world of tech.

I used to wonder why all these spiritual folk used the phrases "mother earth" and "grounding yourself". I was living in what I called "the real world" so I didn't connect with that language. But here's the fact, our bodies and our mother's bodies are made from Earth and once they die they will go back to the earth. We eat foods that come from the earth, and we go to the bathroom each day to remove them from our bodies so they can go back to the earth.

If our physical bodies are not made from the elements of the earth, then what are they made of?

A person eats a lot of food, and they gain weight because they are storing excess earth in their body which hasn't been burnt enough for it to be released.

What do you think we are made of? Cell membrane? Well, what's that? We were not just formed out of nothing. We don't need a science degree to understand the simplicity of it. We are made of the elements, a perfectly mixed cocktail of each.

Our whole body is dependent on the elements, and the periodic table is a part of us rather than some cool thing we study in school. Of the elements, there are five primary ones, like the primary colors. They are earth, wind, fire, water, and ether.

Why do we feel hot? It's the fire being lit inside. Why do we feel cold? It's the cooling system inside us. How can we breathe? Because we take air from the outside in. So put simply, our physical and energetic bodies are made of and rely on the elements.

Furthermore, these elements must have an electrical supply and intelligence working through them. How else would they know how to work together, as well as work with the outside world? I believe this is why life works in perfect harmony, there is a harmonious and intelligent chemistry occurring.

Like a car that has parts, a road that it can drive on, and a generative force that moves through it. That's us, that's life.

Connect to Your Roots — Your Physical

Now that your engine is warmed up, I can really begin explaining the power centres to you by method of how I discovered them for myself.

It started with knowing that I was rooted in the earth like a tree. I remember doing mindfulness meditations where the teacher directed me toward my feet. How weird, I thought, when I bring my attention to my feet and fully focus on them, something interesting happens.

Try it now for 90 seconds.

When I began doing it, I realised the wonder of being aware that my feet are filled with blood, as funny as that sounds. My feet are alive rather than being these things that I walk with and put socks on. Instead of disregarding them, I can cherish the power of these feet which allow me to navigate across this earth.

I remember hearing Thich Nhat Hann saying, "When you walk or run, imagine you are kissing the earth with your feet."

Now I am not into kissing feet (you might be) but when I connected to my feet as electrical conductors that drink the earth's energy, I felt calmer and more grounded, and I was able to get out of my head. Well, that's a useful ability, isn't it?

It literally felt like I was plugging myself into a socket, like when I plug my phone in to charge.

This is because we have an inner power centre that is responsible for our safety and physical well-being. This is what being "grounded" means. How else would our body know we are stable and can relax if we didn't have an intelligent system inside to give us that physical indication? Also, it makes sense that this power centre is physically closest to the earth and connected with our lower body and anus area.

We deposit waste (earth) from this area, back into the earth, so we are quite literally connected with re-soiling the planet. (We would realize this if we lived in the wild). As modern humans, we sit on a toilet rather than coming close to our natural way of excretion. Therefore, we lose touch with the beauty of this process.

There have been numerous occasions during my travels when I had to release my waste out in nature, like in the Peruvian Amazon jungle. As uncomfortable as it felt to my habitual mind, it felt natural to my body.

Anyway, anus aside, the inner potential of the C1 power centre is to feel stable. Whenever I finished a yoga class, I would feel an immense sense of stability because my entire body had become relaxed. The same with a sauna or a massage, the fight or flight response was shut down.

Equally, the issue I was constantly facing (and that most people face) was a feeling of being unsafe. I didn't feel okay in my own skin, and a panic response came up whenever my body was not well rested or when I was overstimulated from a day. I didn't realize that I was overdoing it at times.

The thing with the root centre is that it often turns a situation into life or death; for example when a person cut me off when I was driving, I would feel like they nearly killed me so I would be angry, and then I would carry that anger into my next activity.

Or another example that everyone can relate to is when it comes to money. I found it really hard to spend money in the past because underneath it all was a fear that money may run out. We know logically that it isn't true, but the root centre stops us from really knowing it and spending the money easily.

Therefore a ton of the psycho-physical challenges are connected to the root centre (also intertwining with noise in other centres).

We are connected to animals because we share these feelings of safety and danger. Neuroscience will tell you that we have a reptilian brain, which really is our fight-or-flight response. It's our automatic system that saves us from danger such as a lion growling at us.

I pretty much lived most of my life hyper-vigilant because my alarm systems were constantly signaling threats. A person asking me, "What are you up to this weekend?" would feel like a verbal sword, causing me to tense up and search for an answer that would sound impressive and not be judged.

When sitting in a group of people I would fear being shamed, so I stayed silent and hoped nobody would "attack" me. My sense of safety felt threatened.

It isn't just mental threats though; this centre also holds the intelligence of knowing of what we need for survival. It's the physical tiredness when we are overworked and it's the feeling of safety when wrapped up in a blanket when it's raining outside.

It will not be hard for you to find examples related to the wisdom of the C1 power centre. Try it now. Find 3 examples in your own life which might relate to what you've read so far.

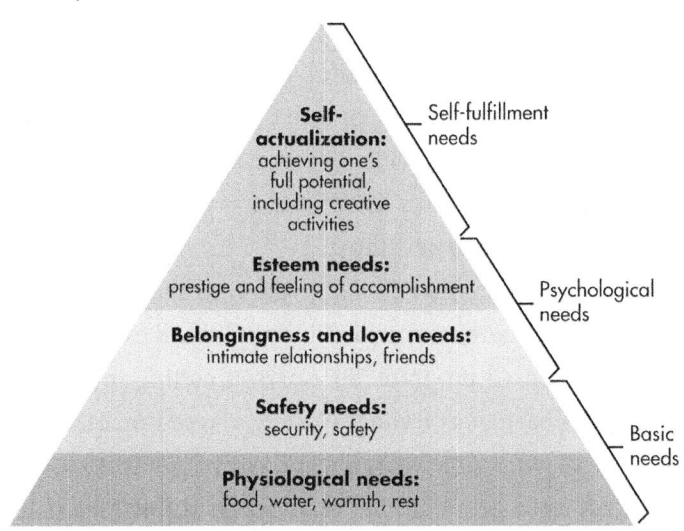

Self-actualization: achieving one's full potential, including creative activities — Self-fulfillment needs

Esteem needs: prestige and feeling of accomplishment — Psychological needs

Belongingness and love needs: intimate relationships, friends

Safety needs: security, safety — Basic needs

Physiological needs: food, water, warmth, rest

Stable or Unstable Responses

As Maslow's famous hierarchy puts it, we need to meet our basic human needs. But it's more complex than purely physical because the mind is involved. The mind creates programs that associate actual danger with emotions and thoughts and stores them in memories. Hence tension can come up in situations that on the surface don't look dangerous, but our minds will tell us they are.

We are more evolved than animals because we have the ability to analyse and self-reflect on a repetitive basis. This ability can turn against us if we feel we are in a situation that poses a risk to our being, our safety, our personality or our "OK'ness", as I like to put it.

We feel the same fear of death during an emotional situation when there is no physical danger in front of us because our mind creates a programmed robot bodyguard who has a steering wheel of their own in our car of life.

I know of many times in my life when I've been trying to drive somewhere in life and the bodyguard suddenly appeared, pushed me out of the seat and pressed the brakes or drove like a maniac. He's paranoid, he thinks someone is following us or trying to hurt us.

There was one time in high school when a girl who liked me used to come and talk to me. She was beautiful, and I liked her too, but I got so intimidated by her that my body went into fight or flight.

I had a choice, let myself feel that or avoid it. I avoided it, and the girl stopped showing interest. That's what I did many times in my life, not just with women but with any opportunity.

Animals know that another animal is about to attack them, so they flee or fight. But for humans, there is an ability to build and live out of a personal identity and event-based program. So a person cutting in front of us in a queue can trigger a barrage of feelings like anger, resentment, or insecurities related to when we were three years old and our parents told us off.

I blocked off kind people in life because I had this idea that I had to prove myself, and at the same time believing that certain types of people cannot be trusted because they could hurt me. I was living in fear and living based on my animal instincts rather than my inner intelligence.

Let me make it clear though–the root centre isn't a bad machine, it is a superpower and a tool.

When fully grounded in the body, when we aren't "tensed up" (as my dad says) we can feel the calm of operating from a stable foundation. The root centre provides a powerful bed of soil for the seed to grow from. It allows for nourishment, it lets in vital energy, and it allows all the energy of the ground and the earth to come into us. We need it to be effective in life. Everything else sits on top of this foundation, so if it's solid, we are stable.

Once I started using my wellbeing practices as a tool for establishing high quality rooting, my whole life began to change. It felt like I was taking in electricity in from the ground and charging my whole body. A great yoga pose that I love is called Warrior One. It opens up the abdomen and chest, it puts the legs into a stance of power and stability, and it's literally like being plugged in, taking in the power of the ground.

Try it, and if you've already tried it, forget what you know and try it for the purpose that I have mentioned in this chapter.

The wellbeing industry has boomed because there are a bunch of people tensed up and trying to calm themselves by overexerting themselves in a workout. I was the same, I often worked out to escape or punish myself, rather than for positive purposes. It was great for the moment, but it left me feeling over-trained and isolated rather than refreshed.

I now understand how to have peak levels of health, body function, and energy levels all year round. This is because I have fundamentally changed how I use my body. If there is less of a fear of safety and more intelligence used, then all the well-being goals in the world can be had. I only realised this once I reconfigured the root centre's energy flow from against me to for me.

Before this, I was constantly undermining myself by eating junk food, junk habits, and junk relationships, all of which were done to try and feel safe inside, something I could have done if I connected to the power of the root instead.

Potential Blocks

The difference between us and animals is that we analyse situations by connecting them to the programming of our self-image and create irrational conclusions. This process consumes a ton of our lifeforce energy, hence why we feel tired when we think too much.

Imagine power centres to be like energy sources, like the plugs around your house. If they are activated, they will consume as much energy as required for a given scenario.

For example, if safety is threatened and the bodyguard's program is switched on, the centres will take energy from all over the body and put the body into a higher functioning mode to ensure that the perceived safety need is met. This is why it becomes so physically demanding to have inner challenges.

I used to feel so drained coming home from social interactions because I was constantly on edge and I only felt relieved if I drank alcohol or if I left. It was like having a safety valve. In university, I used to find a friend to "pre-drink" with before we met the rest of the group because it helped ease my nerves and the knots of tension in my joints.

If the energy is floating around stuck in any centre and isn't able to call in support from the entire system, a person can stay in a loop of fear. The mind will then kick in again to try and look for temporary relief to feel safe. E.g. - food, alcohol, Netflix, sexual release, other people, or whatever it may be for you.

I've tried all those things, and there is absolutely nothing wrong with this, we are human beings. But I am inviting you to be free from them as being compulsive activities that we think we "need". Being driven by my bodily needs is what caused me to play hide and seek for much of my life.

If the energy stays stuck around the root centre and is not able to disperse around and out of the body, then I experienced tension and behaved defensively, irrationally, and in an isolated manner, shutting everything down.

I also discovered that our lifeforce energy will get spent in this one area and there will not be any left for any of the other power centres to use.

Imagine a helium balloon trying to rise to the sky but is being weighed down by a rock and losing its air until it's completely deflated.

The rock is our bodies wanting to go back into the ground. Our bodies are ultimately a piece of earth, and the body knows that its destiny is to die and turn back into earth.

Therefore, if all the energy is focused in the lowest centre of C1 then we will feel slow, uninspired, and heavy. We live like a heavy inactive rock–a lump of flesh, not as a fully-fledged human being.

Our power centres must be all switched on equally for us to be well-balanced in lightness and heaviness. As I said before, we are scientifically a mix of elements, so we need to utilise all of them to effectively become both as strong as a rock and as light as the sky.

Think of it as having 100 dollars each day to spend your energy on, if you are spending 90 dollars in only one energy playground then there's hardly anything left to channel any energy towards others.

Unfortunately, a huge chunk of people will be stuck spending all their money here (I sure did). It's the reason we hold back on things outside of safety, things like spending money (a big one) and how we treat our bodies. If the body is spending all its time trying to detox the junk inside or trying to come to a place of recovery and good health, then there's not much left for the things outside of that.

That's why health is so important; the root centre working at its best requires our bodies to be well-kept, because it is the body.

The key point to mention is that the mind can mislead us into thinking that the body signals are bad. I was stuck in this for a long time. I used my body as a barometer for what is "bad" or "good" and based my actions off this conclusion.

I thought that alert signals meant bad, and that calmness meant good. Now I have realised that the root centre is just giving me signals, I don't need to buy into a mental story about it, and I don't need to stop myself from doing things because of it.

The challenge I faced was that my mind added a layer to everything, and a small tension created bigger tension, which might have grown into a subtle or gross level of overwhelm.

The best piece of advice I can give you here is to ease and nurture the body. Slow it down as much as you can so that you can be in command of it. The mind usually feels less noisy when the body is compliant, and when it isn't throwing fuel into the fire. I keep a physical practice each morning to help me get into my body and to observe the mind, rather than reacting based on it.

It starts with keeping the body well, which is why yoga has physical postures, to help us harmonise the nervous system so that it isn't jumpier than it needs to be. From that place, we are rooted with a healthy foundation, and we can ascend and use the rest of the system better.

It's also why meditation is traditionally meant to be practiced after yoga postures and breathing exercises, because after postures the body is more compliant and not getting in the way of us. I followed that formula for many years and I began to experience a level of calm that I hadn't felt in my entire life. My body started to feel safer, rather than feeling like I had to stay so vigilant in situations.

To Summarise

The root centre (C1) grounds us into our physical nature, but too much grounding and we are in the ground, alive yet dead. We have nothing to keep us ascending upwards. The balloon of our existence cannot float. In the next chapters, we will start exploring the next rungs of the ladders toward that floating.

Remember though, lower isn't bad, it's a requirement for the higher centres to work at their best. Like the roots of a tree and a base of a pyramid, we need a strong physical frame to work with. Stability, that's C1, the root centre's power.

✏️ Questions to consider:

What types of situations or circumstances give you a true sense of being grounded?

What takes it away and sends you into a sense of pessimism, concern, or fight or flight?

What does having stability feel like to you?

What physical practices are most helpful and least helpful for your overall well-being?

What could you experiment with based on what you've read?

Wisdom 101 - The Power of Unifying Oneself

"In oneself lies the whole world, and if you know how to look and learn, the door is there and the key is in your hand."
~ Jiddu Krishnamurti

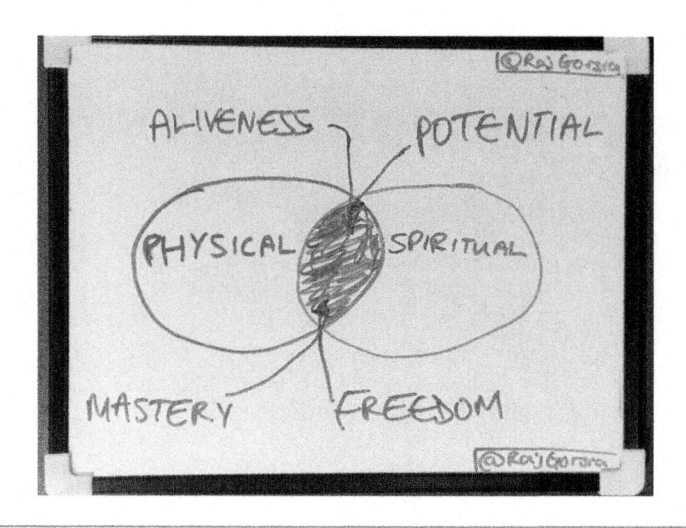

Let's pause our ascension journey for a moment to discuss Yogic wisdom based on my current understanding.

In spiritual sciences such as Yoga, Taoism, Tantra, and Hermeticism–among others–there is the concept of having two major connecting forces that govern everything. In fact, even neuroscience will say the same, although neuroscience usually relates it to a personal body, rather than a universal system.

That could be a way to define "spiritual science". It's universal, rather than personal.

In ancient Taoism these two forces are Yin and Yang, in Indian Tradition it is Shiva and Shakti, and in Hermeticism there is the Above and Below. There are also many other traditions that have a similar way of describing it.

In my opinion, they are all saying the same thing, like a thousand people trying to explain what aliveness is, each of them may have a different way of describing it, but they all lead to the same place.

My experiences have heavily been focused on the Yogic Shiva/Shakti framework. It has made so much sense to me because it's an embodied, felt, and lived experience, through the practice of yoga and life rather than an intellectual-based philosophy.

I have always been into embodiment practices because they feel the most realistic. I don't need to think about what's true, I feel it. Logic has only ever taken me deeper into the maze of the mind and tickled my ego, whereas felt experience takes me to a place of true understanding.

The Twin Flame

Lifeforce power is Shakti, and Consciousness is Shiva. Shakti is moving and Shiva is still. One is the aliveness and the other is the nothingness. It's a natural cycle, every bit of science and every bit of life is formed off these two principles. Modern scientists will have their own way of looking at it.

The Shakti power is always wanting to unite with Shiva because the joining of the forces creates a state of ultimate bliss, empowerment, and peace. It creates a whirlwind of a force that is like no other, a force unattainable if the two are on their own. Performance experts may relate this to flow.

The famous image of Yin and Yang shows a tiny white circle in the black part and a tiny black one in the white part. It's not there to make the image look nice, it's there on purpose to show us that they both have a piece of each other in them, and that they are one of the same.

I also think that they put a hole in each to remind us that we must join the two in order to experience the full potential of life.

It's like having two puzzle pieces that fit perfectly on top of each other. When you put them together wouldn't you feel this euphoric experience of completion and joy? It's this same satisfying feeling that we get when we join the two forces of life together.

When I started creating experiences where I was unifying the forces of life together, I felt a feeling of total obliteration of tension, raw clarity, and aliveness. Like seeing a sunrise at a mountain, it leaves you awestruck, and pure silence possesses the body.

No wonder the feeling of two humans getting intimate is extremely pleasurable; it was designed to encourage us to learn how the greater puzzle pieces of life are meant to fit together.

I would sit there smiling at trees throughout my day when I was in this state of union, even using a pen would feel like ultimate bliss, I was amazed at how cool everything was.

Sometimes I'd burst out into hysterical laughter like I had been smoking drugs, it would last a few minutes at least, and during the day a trace of it would remain sprinkled into my way of operating.

This experience also resulted in getting into such a hyper-focused clarity that something which usually took me two hours would be happening in twenty minutes. I had instant access to genius, calm and aliveness.

All of this was happening because I could literally feel the physical and energetic chemistry of these two forces joining together. I would be walking down the street and see kids laughing and I would feel ultimate love for them even if they are strangers. My heart would expand and melt at the same time. The idea of "Raj Gorsia" dissolves, the idea of separation dissolved too, and everything became one.

Guess what. You have experienced what I am saying in some way, trust me. Pause for one minute and think of a time, right now.

* * *

It feels like the highest state, doesn't it? And guess what happens in this state? We do not need this idea of self-love anymore, because the idea of self has disappeared, we are no longer alone or separate. And yet we can still experience everything from the popcorn enjoying movie seat of perceived separateness.

It's like a wave that channels the raw power of the entire ocean but still enjoys the mode of being a separate wave.

That's the level of freedom and empowerment that I am inviting you to explore more of as you read the rest of this book.

It's real, this ain't no spiritual voodoo or mythical dream, it's the DNA of life that people from Einstein to Buddha knew, the same thing that modern scientists know, and the same thing that deep down we all know…Beyond our psychological mind.

Know *Beyond* Thy-Self

The lifeforce power is said to reside around the root centre (C1), from my personal experiences I would say it really explodes its potential around the creative centre (C2). As I said, the rooting system we have within us is like a tree that takes its source of energy from the outside.

The earth takes its energy from its source, like how our cells are a part of an organ, and an organ a part of the body. The universal hierarchy seems to work in the same way. Logical, right?

The ability to transform this source of energy into a personal experience happens through the systems of the C1 (1st centre) and can be amplified via the C2 (2nd centre).

This ultimate source of electrical power flows through us and wants to work its way through the other power centres, all the way up through the third eye centre (C6) where it can meet its ultimate destiny.

It's like having a magnet; wouldn't the magnet experience massive satisfaction when it touches the other side of a pole? Our poles are far apart like the poles of earth, and it's necessary for our machinery to be built this way. But still, the magnetic bond creates a natural yearning for unity.

You will notice this desire and pleasure in unity happening in some shape or form in your life.

For example, going into nature gives us energy, but we can only enjoy it when we are present and conscious of its awe, taking in the whole experience of it. That right there is an example of high energy meeting high awareness to create bliss. Whether we realise it or not (hopefully now you will) we are naturally wired to yearn for a union between polarities in life.

I have gone into nature and have been stuck with wrestling the racing thoughts in my head, and guess what? I did not experience any peace or bliss. It was like being a robot stomping around in the green without feeling the present moment's joy of it. Can you relate?

The same thing has happened when I have been sitting with friends and I've been using my phone; I am not conscious of the energy of aliveness moving through me, I am not tapping into the possibility of easy bliss in that moment. So the body feels dull because junk presence is like eating junk food.

That is what I mean when I say Shiva-Shakti, yin-yang, above-below etc. They work best as a pair, like two dancers. They are meant to be together, so there is always a natural seeking to be together.

And we are in the middle of both, we have the power to join the two worlds and wield both their powers, which means wielding the power centres within us. Our systems of operation.

One Of The Same

The heart is the central headquarters (more on the heart later) and it's the power that allows the polar energies and all the power centres (and any aspect of life) to merge. Love is the power or the glue that allows for the combination of all things.

Think about it.

What allows you to be so enthused by a task? Or infatuated by a person or a TV show?

It's a melting and a union, with love being the dissolving chemical that allows for barriers to melt. Otherwise, we'd be robots and we would see pictures on the TV but would be numb and feel nothing inside of ourselves. We need a transmitter, and that's the heart's job.

I say that heart takes us from ME to WE. It takes us beyond our separateness, which can ultimately lift the veil on most of our fears. It allows us to be personal and universal at the same time. The wave and the ocean. It connects two worlds–exactly the reason why it's located in the middle of us.

The tricky part is that we can naturally stay in the guarded stance of separateness, which is the function of the psychological and self-preserving mind.

Nothing is wrong with that, I am not talking about the morals of right and wrong, and I am not talking about shaming ourselves "oh that's me, I am so bad". Bad doesn't exist, as everything has its function in our lives. Awareness is the focus, so you can feel how the car is being driven.

We need to be able to function separately, as long as we don't limit our true potential because of it. I did that, I blocked off a ton of people because I was seeing such a distinct difference between me and them, rather than seeing the unification through our similarities.

It's About Potential

I hope what you've read so far will prime you as we continue this journey. Let it sink in before you continue, because the rest of the journey will be about the incredible story of Shakti (the lifeforce power) journeying through the centres to meet Shiva (the source) at the top.

Think of each centre as a pit stop and an upgrade in levels of potential that you can unlock from inside you. Like a game. As the kundalini (another word for lifeforce) energy rises through the power centres, the game of life gets more exciting and fulfilling.

The power centres hold our fullest potential as humans. In fact, our body is already using them throughout every experience of our lives. Even a neuroscientist could tell you that, though they might use more "sciency" words. So we may as well understand how to use them consciously and optimally rather than being in the dark.

It's like living in a house that has a library with the secrets to life. The challenge is that you either never knew that the room was there, or you see the books but don't understand them or know how to apply them. The words might be in a complicated or alien language.

Don't worry–it need not be over-complicated, it's simpler than many of the spiritual folk or the science folk out there might make it out to be.

These abilities are your natural birthright; it's already within you, it is not something that we don't have. Like your voice. We all have one, but we can use it at varying degrees.

* * *

All-Wheel Drive

It might sound biased, but yogic practices fascinate me most because they are so extensive and colorful, covering the entire spectrum of human science. I have also been influenced by Hermeticism, Buddhism, Taoism and Zen. In the end, all teachings seem to be speaking about the same things: the ending of disunity.

Let me be clear though, the focus of this writing is to talk about life wisdom, but not from a place of aligning to any one religion. I'd rather not align with any association if I can gain the benefits from them all.

The word yoga means to unite, to "yoke" together. If you whisk an egg, it turns into a mixture that is no longer white or yolk. That is what I love to do and wish to invite you towards.

I have gone down the route of figuring out how to mix physical fitness with spiritual awakening and mind mastery. To me, this has been a fun game of mixing things together to make cocktails that are tastier when mixed together versus separate.

Have you ever tried a date, banana, spinach, and mango smoothie? It's one of my favorites. It's amazing because it combines a lot of vitamins and flavors together. I make all sorts of smoothie combinations and food combinations. Imagine how food would be without mixing things together.

It's the same with the power centres, as with skills and experience. If you are a confident speaker who is also very empathetic, imagine how powerfully you can impact people with your voice. If you are highly strategic as well as fearless in your actions, then you will get stuff done.

That's what true yoga (unifying) is to me; living it, not just on a cute soft matt, but in the real world. Driving through these centres, and driving with all wheels, just feels nice as a metaphor, doesn't it?

* * *

Let's Get Ready To Rumble

Keep any insights that you've gathered so far in your awareness as you continue to read. The story of our energetic potential is going to be laid out through a journey of curiosity, courage, and intelligence–with Shakti (lifeforce power) moving through each of the power centres along the way.

Read it as a fairy tale and a legendary story. Story hits us in a unique way, doesn't it? I honestly think that religions laid it in stories so that it overrides our analytical brain and really lands for us. Smart.

And the most exciting part is that this story is about you. Do not forget that as you read each word.

There are characters that you have been and will become. There are pit stops that you face, there is intelligence and there is a mystery.

But it's all about you, please keep reminding yourself of that because it will allow you to experience this journey in a unique way. A way that will ultimately lead you to use the forces within you as tools for your life rather than something you need to mentally buy into.

This path was never a belief that I had to intellectually buy into, it's always an ongoing experiment and evolution of life experience.

My invitation is to see if you can do the same.

Let's put the keys into the ignition and get going on this ride.

I encourage you to pause in between each chapter, like having a rest at a pit stop.

✏️ Questions to consider:

What spiritual and psychological beliefs have you been exposed to and how have they influenced the way you see the world?

_____
_____
_____
_____
_____

What other ways of looking at things have you been curious about?

_____
_____
_____
_____
_____

What do you really want in life?

_____
_____
_____
_____
_____

C2 - The Creative Centre — The Power of Being You

Chakra Name: *Swadhistana*
Sanskrit Meaning: *Place of Self*
Location: *Sacrum*
Elemental Power: *Water*

"A creative life is an amplified life. It's a bigger life, a happier life, an expanded life, and a hell of a lot more interesting life"
~ Elizabeth Gilbert

I drew this in Egypt at an art therapy session

All of the power centres connect to each other, like a train track. The activation of one of them will ultimately amplify the power of the next one. Having said that, my experience tells me that we do not need to work through each centre systematically in a fixed order. Instead, I see them like instruments in a symphony.

We all have different levels of development that have naturally occurred (consciously or unconsciously) within each centre. It's not a pre-requisite or formulaic process to go through them one by one. This is where some people may get lost, thinking that each centre is independent.

Instead think of each as a part of a system, like a soup with different spices or an orchestra that works together to create wonderful music.

If you get too focused on intellectually separating your power centres then you might miss the entire purpose of this journey and life's journey.

My way of seeing life's journey is seeing the unity of one with all. The parts of a car with the whole car. It fascinates me to understand and master each part of life, but it fascinates me more to see how things work together to create an even greater power.

I spent a lot of my childhood watching my handyman dad pick things apart, like parts of a car. Working on them and then putting them together again. I didn't know it at the time, but the engineer in him is in me too, it just manifests in a slightly different way.

The Creative Spark Plug Of Your Car

The C2 centre is connected to the sexual energy and our potency as humans. So to stay in tune with my simple way of speaking (if you haven't noticed it already), this power source represents our potential to create. Not just create physical life forms but create anything.

From my experience, Shakti's power (the lifeforce) resides dormant around this area and equally has the potential to explode from this area. Once I ignited the power within this area, I started noticing that I became more creative in my outlook and approach to life.

I spent most of my life believing that creativity was for left-handed artsy people, because I never really understood or felt creative and it never seemed to come to me over the years. I would look at a painting and see colors and that's it. No depth to my awareness, no excitement or personal interpretation, like a robot.

I separated myself from those who dance, who paint, who write, and who sing. They were not "my kind of people", my kind of people were strength-driven, achievement-driven, hedonistic, tech people, or highly intellectual.

Once I sparked this creative force inside me, I was able to feel the energy that goes into all of creation, beyond art. I understood how beautiful it is to see rainfall, to see the plants grow and the birds sing. I started seeing that all of these natural phenomena are a result of the creative force of life dancing in the physical form. I felt the juice of life flowing inside and outside of me.

I saw that the artists I said were not my people, were in fact my people because I saw that I was that person too. I was born out of that force of power, so how could I not be that type of person?

I became more open with others, I was seeing things with a fresh pair of eyes, unafraid to forget the old, and ready to explore the new. My eyes started to glow like I was a kid again, so excited and imaginative. Ready to feel things that I never knew I could feel.

In my opinion, C2 is a fun superpower to wield. It brings a primal energy into us that exudes excitement. It's removing the covering and showing the real us, without shame. Allowing the juice to move us.

Why do you think it feels so good to procreate? (F word if you prefer!) Because the juices of life are flowing through us. People have sex with people and then regret it in the morning, why? Because they were being allured by the energy of intimacy in the moment.

Wielding the power of C2 is thrilling because it allows us to feel who we are as a flow of energy rather than an intellectual idea. It unlocks something that the logical mind cannot replicate.

It's funny, I noticed that C2 is so far away from the head in terms of location and thought to myself that they must have designed it that way for a reason. Whatever made us humans knew what it was doing, down to the geometry of our bodies.

Every business owner, adventure seeker and artist has tapped into this centre's potential at one point. It's what allowed them to birth the idea.

A womb and a penis are where humans come from, so doesn't it make sense that our creative energy comes from the same area? We literally create and give birth to our ideas by first sparking a burst of energy.

Both men and women are using a metaphorical magical wand and casting spells through their words and behaviors. The juice that drives it must come from somewhere, right?

That's the question I began asking myself, and the answer brought me to the words I am sharing with you.

Every creator will struggle to explain their inspiration. They will just say, "I just felt it" or "it came to me". I started to see that everything that's ever been made was made by a creative genius beyond the person.

During my meditation practices, I ran some experiments and I started to observe that this creative force came from the personal intake of lifeforce from a higher force that is beyond the personal.

I noticed that I had a system inside me that took in this higher force and transformed it from universal to personal (it comes into me) through the technology within the creative centre.

I also saw that when C1 (the root centre) is stabilised, the creative energy feels way freer in revealing itself, meaning Shakti (the primal power) can unleash and push her power through my body.

If the fear of physical safety is out of the way, then the flow of the pipe is clear. Otherwise, it cuts itself off, like a safety switch on a light that automatically cuts out after certain conditions occur.

The very idea of becoming a guide to others started when my creative centre began opening.

I remember feeling my energy oozing out of my skin, as a signal to say, "Hey you got to do this, and this is what you must do". Everything clicked, the juice was gushing out, and ideas were flowing through me. This juice led me towards a collection of ideas and actions to take towards them.

The rest is history. Here I am today writing this book. Sparked, a potency moving through me as I write.

Sensitivity For The Good

Once you really understand this for yourself and start using this flow of energy as a tool, you will have the ability to be creative and transform any area of your life.

When I began channeling the power of C2 more effectively, I noticed my sexual and eating desires transform from being overly pleasure-seeking to aliveness-seeking. An intuitive compass was emerging.

I became slimmer, eliminated cravings, had more radiant skin, and my overall health became sweeter because there was less fear and hiding of myself.

I felt way more inspired to live my life fully and to connect with people on an energetic level. It's so funny to say this, but I felt like I unlocked the glow that pregnant women get. Where do you think it comes from? They are full of creative energy.

The lust I often craved for pleasure was transmuted into a newfound desire for exploration, I began choosing things in my life that I felt energized by, rather than what I thought would help me on paper.

Less mentally driven decisions, and more energetic. I dropped some of the expectations to be "a good" human, and the shame of not fitting in.

* * *

For most of my life, I tried to fit in and I felt emotionally hurt every time I felt left out. Opening the power (or flower) of this centre allowed me to become excited to finally explore what being me was, the me that I forgot existed. That flower, that intimate part of me.

Kundalini yoga practices definitely helped me with this, along with zen practices, precise health and fitness disciplines, understanding psychology and neuroscience, and freeing my inner child.

Once everything aligns, the energy that gushes out of us is one of such potency, like a 100% proof alcohol, tiny measures of this force can create massive waves of transformation.

It's like hitting the jackpot of potential. Like hitting a switch in a car and the engine is injected with a fluid that is so potent the car begins to move with more oomphf, with as little as a few drops injected.

It makes sense though doesn't it; an egg and a sperm that has the power to create life are generated here, so the creative centre *has* to contain the most sophisticated algorithm and source code to create anything. It must have enough oomphf for life to burst out of it.

What would it feel like if you had more oomphf?

What could be possible for your life?

What gets in the way?

Ask yourself these questions before continuing.

Potential Blocks

If there are blocks due to fear of safety around the root centre, then we will not want to create any new ideas because the psychology of "What's the point?" might come up.

What I mean by this is that if I am under the illusion that my ideas are worthless and unlikely to be successful, and if I am trapped in the cycle of a mind storm then I will not even be able to see any possibilities for "newness". From this place, I can't begin to fully utilize the powers from the team in the creative centre.

It's like when you ask your friend to come to a concert with you and they say, "No that's expensive" or… "No, it's dangerous". Your passion is killed instantly. The root centre can destroy our creativity instantly because it's overly concerned with staying safe.

The survival element of the mind is frozen in the belief that there is a possibility of losing something, therefore it deems the idea unworthy of action. That dialogue goes on in us sometimes, either consciously or unconsciously.

This was the biggest challenge throughout my life. I have had moments where I was so trapped in my own doubt that I could not even think of the possibility of anything other than negativity.

An ex-girlfriend used to say to me, "All is black in your eyes; you aren't Raj anymore, you are gone." She was right, I was so trapped inside my head that I shut her out, shut myself out, and wanted to curl up into a ball.

Like going back into the womb as a fetus again, reverse-aliveness. Even though on the outside or through my language, I looked like I was taking a noble stand and I was able to function properly, the glow of light left my skin and my guard went up. Like a stern ghost.

Feeling unsafe keeps us in the trap of the root centre, the animal mind. The creative centre allows clean water to come through the pipes, if it is feeling blocked then the pipes get dry and life feels dooming, that's how it felt for me anyway.

The Filters To The Flow

The creative centre is the place where the exploration of energy happens, it must be why people wish to experiment with drugs and with their sexuality. We as humans love to explore the world through the mode of felt energy rather than just our analytical mind.

I travel around the world because I love to experience the bounce of aliveness in different forms.

When I traveled to Thailand for my first solo trip I was buzzing with energy. As much as I enjoyed the nightlife, I was more invested and drawn to the cultural experiences. And beyond that, I loved the experience of life itself; people watching, watching myself, patting myself on the back for even going there. Feeling it, smelling it, taking it all in.

I have traveled through life impulsively taking actions because on certain occasions I feel a passionate energy moving me which overrides my logical reasons not to act. Those decisions are usually the most exciting ones.

Higher development of this freedom-based living began opening up when I created space in all of the other centres, which we will get to...

The stronger our flow, the more we can allow ourselves to get excited by life and push the energy into the other power centres to power-stack (like skill stacking) which further amplifies our abilities.

If you find your flow getting blocked by shame or embarrassment, then it might be due to C2 being constricted. A special part of you hidden away.

* * *

The Shame Game

I had a heavy fear of being embarrassed because I was the youngest child and I interpreted myself as being looked down on for most of my life. I felt like I was told how to be, so I built this program within myself that it is not okay to be just me.

It felt shameful to fully express myself, my subconscious said that I must be a "good boy" in order to avoid rejection, which in my young psychology translated to avoiding death itself. It felt better to hide and avoid being laughed at or risk the pain of being told off and feeling like "I am wrong (as a human)".

This stuck with me for most of my life, so I lost touch with this dancer, speaker, playful and funny part inside me. I lived tense because being less serious literally felt like it could open up a threat into my world such as "messing things up" or "being wrong".

Deep down I had this innate desire to be an inspiration to people. But my identity was one of powerlessness and weakness, so I suppressed the innate passion I had, and I held back. It sucked because it meant that this energy didn't get a chance to move through me or develop.

It was locked in exile, and I threw away the keys. Some may relate this to the "inner child", but that phrase can be misunderstood and get too heady, so let's keep it energetic and call it the "golden glow".

Being expressive (this golden glow) felt shameful and painful deep down inside, so I created an identity that unconsciously condemned it and blocked it off.

When I began to rediscover and reconnect to this part of me, tears, grief, and resentment flooded through my being over some months because it felt like I had rediscovered a betrayed, beautiful, and forever innocent version of myself.

But as I like to say to others, there's a difference between tears of entrapment and tears of liberation. My tears were definitely of pure liberation and unshackling.

I realised that I could now be friends with my golden glowing self and let him out to express himself.

It felt like removing the knot in the hose pipe that was blocking the flow of water, so my whole way of operating became smoother. Emotional freedom is a term that some might use.

I have sent some of my clients the song "smooth operator" by Sade. I have told them to listen to it over and over again and notice what it would be like to be a smooth operator in life.

Not cognitively, but as a rhythm, as a way of dancing through life. To really feel the energy flood through them and move with it.

Being a smooth operator means operating with a spring in our step, like someone who's just got lucky and is suddenly overly friendly and joyful, having what we call "a good day".

Well why wait for that good day to occur based on outside circumstances, when we can produce that energy as an inside job, any time we want. That's what I set out to do, to really master how to release the stagnant energy and produce a fresh new flow of it, at will.

The body contains the codes, but first the seed must be planted and the button must be pressed. I hope that my writing is doing that for you, to trigger a decision to free more of yourself.

To start with, find the song "Smooth Operator" and listen with the ears of your energy. Try on the outfit of being a smooth operator and then ask yourself these questions:

What does it feel like to be smooth in your flow?

What would be possible if you were even smoother in different areas of your life? List out each area and note down whatever comes up.

How To Unlock Your Superpowers

I want to touch on the topic of guidance before I continue. I am not going to give you a step-by-step list of "doings" in this book. I could do that, but this book is more about understanding and shifting your way of seeing things.

I am not implying that reading this book will not provide some "how to's", it most certainly will, either directly through my prompts or indirectly, through you. The thing I've realised, is that empowerment is most important.

If I told you how to cut a tree but your energy isn't in it, if you aren't empowered, then it doesn't matter if you've got the technique, you will not cut a tree like a person who's enthused. Now scale that same manner of operating into every area of your life, in every moment, every day. What's the effect?

So look out for those energy shifts and those insights, they will create ongoing micro-tears of transformation in you. It's like muscle building, micro shifts in operating create more micro-tears in the muscle. Add precise tweaks to the process, and the results are exponential.

Remember, one of my roles is to be a fire starter, I am here to spark your fireworks. I am talking to your creative centre right now and seeing if it can listen. Can it?

Don't even look at me as special. The outer guide's purpose is to lead you toward your inner guide. I am here to point you in the right direction, help you to stay on the path, and swerve you away from the directions that are superficial.

You will know the difference, inside you. It's like driving a car anxiously versus driving the car with ease…

And as with every car, it is often useful to see what's under the hood. So let's continue this ride toward the next centre…C3, which I call "The Launch Pad". The journey is about to get exciting. You will even notice that the energy I write the next chapter with is different from this one. But before we go there…

✏️ Questions to consider:

What types of situations or circumstances give you a feeling of passionate power?

Now give me a deeper answer, what really does it? When do you feel taken over by the lifeforce within you, to a level where you are "positively possessed"?

What keeps you away from it?

What filter/mask/fear comes up that holds you back from being fully emotive?

What did this chapter spark inside you that you'd like to experiment with in your life?

C3 - The Core Centre - The Power To Launch

Chakra Name: *Manipura*
Sanskrit Meaning: *Jewel Storehouse*
Location: *Solar Plexus*
Elemental Power: *Fire*

"Just like in bodybuilding, failure is also a necessary experience for growth in our own lives, for if we're never tested to our limits, how will we know how strong we really are? How will we ever grow."
~ Arnold Schwarzenegger

In physical fitness, we talk about "the core" as this sexy six-pack that models have. People will see a six-pack as a representation of inner accomplishment because it's one of the hardest things to craft. I got drawn into this world myself because I used bodybuilding as a method for trying to build confidence within myself.

Looking in the mirror and working on my body gave me a feeling of "I am okay", "I am strong", and "Wow, I actually have some power to change something, I am not stuck with what I was given". It was really useful for that purpose at the time.

But I also discovered the truth bomb that there is no true satisfaction in physical appearance alone, no matter how good the body looks. I saw that the inner ego is judging and striving for some kind of idea of what it thinks perfect is, and the body can be used as an avenue to try and feel that idea of perfection. One of many.

Don't get me wrong, I still keep my body at its peak because it's useful as a catalyst for my overall life potential to explode, but it is quite different from a physical focus alone, which can become an unhealthy addiction. It's like using money to try to feel happy, like believing that having a vitamin supplement will allow you to access a shortcut toward wellbeing (I did that one).

The number of people depressed and punishing themselves because of their physical looks is larger than we think, even people who in our opinion may seem physically breathtaking. I realised this for myself after a lifetime of obsessing in front of the mirror, staring at my overly skinny body, my obese body, and my muscular body (I've been through all the phases and four different t-shirt sizes.)

I had a body that most would be happy with, but I was not satisfied. I was desperate for more. More muscle, less fat, heavier weights to lift, better running personal bests, physical performance, endurance, more nutritional knowledge, more rituals, and more supplements to take.

Then one day I asked myself - why? Why, does, this, not, satisfy me? And… what is the true point of this?

No matter how good the physical flesh looks, there is a person inside who just wants to be free and live a fully expressed life. Somewhere deep down there is a tiny flame, which is massive in power…

* * *

Activate Your Core

C3 is a powerful centre that can allow us to experience our full expression because it is related to the power source inside us. It's like a battery pack, connecting us to our digestive system and our sense of strength. It works both internally and externally, although I'd suggest that both worlds are one and the same.

It's the furnace, transforming the fuel from outside of the body into a usable internal power source. It also supplies energy towards activating modes of operation such as courage. It allows for the readiness and transfer of energy for a person to take action in life. A strong will comes from here.

Food goes to this area, twisting your body comes from this area, so it makes sense that it is called "The Core" isn't it? But not just the core in terms of physical, as the personal trainer calls it. I mean the core as a cauldron of possibilities, a fuel for life. A fuel that not only allows us to survive, but to flourish and mobilise both internally and externally.

I began noticing its power when I was doing powerful breath practices such as "the breath of fire", kundalini kriyas, as well as demanding abdominal exercises and high-intensity programs such as power lifting or sprinting.

The core has to be fully activated for our fullest power to spread throughout the body, into the arms, the legs, filling the lungs, moving blood, and activating the whole body.

Again, both as an internal action and external action. Kriya yoga is internal action, and karma yoga is external action. Both cause an effect. I practice living by both paths because I have found that a combination of both is required to reach my absolute potential. When inside and outside match, I am most empowered and free.

Activating the core centre is like throwing more wood into a fire, hell it's like a tank of gasoline is thrown in too. When I discovered this, I began to explode in my levels of output. I was exercising more powerfully than ever when I learned how to directly activate the core more efficiently. Not just physical exercise though, my cognitive ability was focused and I was able to take action that I was scared to take with more fire and confidence.

Can you feel that spinning fire wheel inside of your belly? One of my favorite fireworks as a kid was the Catherine wheel. That's what you have inside of you–that's what the power centres are. They are like finding different types of fountains of youth and wormholes of possibilities.

Pause for two minutes and bring your awareness to this region of your body and get in touch with everything I have described so far. What do you notice? There is no right answer, but your own experience.

"You Are A Walking Talking Firestorm"

This is the line I recited to remind myself of my power during a time when I was struggling to take action and getting stuck in my head. I also said it to one of my clients, as I helped her engage her fiery core and show up to her next activities with unstoppable confidence.

The sun is powerful, and we are a little version of it.

> *"Keep your face always toward the sunshine*
> *—and shadows will fall behind you."*
> ~ Walt Whitman

Indians, Mexicans, Egyptians, and other cultures have been aware that we have a very intimate relationship with the sun. They created specific rituals and systems based on it. They utilised the sun in an intelligent way to create prosperity in their lives. Read up on it to learn more.

They didn't have the internet that we have now, and they were able to advance. They created wisdom that is still useful for modern cultures today.

And hey I don't just look at that and say wow, cool historical fact. Yeah that's nice and all, but instead, it's way more useful to look into myself and see how I can access the same wisdom for myself. If they can do it, why can't I? If anyone can do anything, why can't I?

My father will tell you that I always used to like playing with all his tools, 8-year-old me walking around with his axe and chopping the skin off the trees to see what's underneath them. Or finding his screwdrivers and opening random things up with it. I have always been fascinated with knowing how things work inside.

So I do the same with my life, testing practices to see what would happen, mixing potions, running experiments. I encourage you to do the same.

Through my felt-experience, I can clearly say that the core centre is like having the sun inside our stomachs. Doing certain yoga routines like sun salutations and kundalini breath practices activates the solar-powered battery in my body.

Doing them, you will instantly notice a feeling of strength, courage, and clarity. (Check my YouTube or other peoples for instructional videos)

The heat will rise in your body and you will feel a sense of alertness equivalent to having a strong cappuccino. Why take drugs like caffeine when you can create a cleaner and purer energy from inside right? That's the question I asked myself anyway.

* * *

As with every centre, the solar centre powerfully connects to the lower centres. If we are feeling grounded in C1 and potently creative in C2, then the core (C3) can supply more fuel and provide a mechanism for bursting our energy out in the world.

It's like the flamethrower and the flame, the gasoline (lifeforce) moves through our body through the sex organs (the C2 zone). The physical body is rooted into the ground and centred in the core in order to hold and use the flamethrower.

Ever tried using a flamethrower? I haven't, but use your imagination for a moment and try to imagine it. And then imagine the flamethrower, the person holding it, and the flame–at the same time. They need to work together as a car works with parts. There also has to be a drive to pull the trigger, the core provides the will to pull the trigger.

The core supports the ability for our energy to be used for either restoration, preservation, or action. It can move us either upwards or downwards, sideways, or diagonally, both physically and metaphorically. A personal trainer will tell you that there are multi-dimensional purposes of the core.

I myself became a certified personal trainer and I remember the course materials always talking about the core and our energy systems. But I am now taking you beyond the physical realm, whilst also including the physical. I am all about the physical science, the neuroscience, and the spiritual science, combining them to hit many dimensions of our life at once.

Once you really understand how to use this power centre, you can use it for whatever purpose you want–health, action taking, accessing different energy states, creating success, whatever you want. A tank full of rocket fuel can fly you to a lot of places.

I started to think, how cool is it to have that kind of power over my life? For a guy who was used to beating himself up and bullying himself into shame and discouragement, it was pretty amazing for me to learn how to turn the rockets on.

The thing is, how this fire sparks can either happen consciously with poise or unconsciously (psychological autopilot) where the energy and focus are thrown all over the place.

I like to call it a wild fire, as opposed to a controlled fire. The flamethrower throwing the person into flames or the person mastering the flame and sending it in whatever direction the person wishes.

Have you ever seen a rocket spinning in all directions? It's quite stressful to be around. Versus a rocket that launches straight up without wasting energy on anything else. That's what we are looking for, switching from non-directed fire to directed fire, a missile with clear co-ordinates, roaring through the sky.

* * *

For most of my life, the flame was my worst enemy, fight or flight mode and my body believed that I had to prove something to myself. This whole ego thing came upon me, and it manifested in me judging myself or others. I rarely expressed it outwardly, but instead I felt inner anger because my core centre was getting into war mode. I was the spinning rocket for sure, energy turning against itself.

Can you relate to what I've been saying so far? Take a moment and think of times when you have thrown yourself into flames and compare with times when you have been able to wield your flame confidently, even in the tiniest of ways.

Here's one that used to come up for me a lot. Whenever there was an opportunity to speak to someone or to use my voice to say something, I would hesitate, hold back and then judge myself for it. It's like the flame was burning me from the inside rather than me ushering it to come out.

I remember being in school talking to a girl, let's call her Sarah. She kept coming near me, wanting to know me. I stood there like a stone statue and didn't say anything. I almost wanted her to go away to avoid the embarrassment of not being able to stand confidently.

This has happened to me over and over with women, with work colleagues, friends, family, sports, job opportunities, life opportunities–with anything really. I wasn't being in my present moment power, I wasn't carpe diem'ing.

I wasn't showing my flame, so the flame was turning against me with physical and mental suffering. It was telling me through inner signals, saying "hey, you are powerful, you know... don't put that fire out". But at the same time, my subconscious mind was telling me "Hey you aren't good enough, this situation proved it, again..."

The same thing happened whenever I faced confrontation. I blamed myself and didn't stand up for myself. I didn't let the fire in me move when someone was trying to hurt me or shame me. I was bullied a little while growing up, so I must have decided that it's easier to wait for it to be over, play dead and keep it all in, rather than stand strong.

The same happened when I was around people who were high energy and dominant. I would play the role of "pleaser" and go into the nice guy mode. Nod along, go along and forget my own values in the process.

You know how much these situations suck right?

Wielding the flame unlocks the ability to become a walking talking firestorm. That's the only phrase that came to me when I began feeling my flame. It felt empowering; I am a firestorm, confident, powerful, strong, and unshakable.

It isn't a cute phrase or an affirmation that magically came true because I told it to myself. The practices that I did with my body's energy and the actions I took allowed for me to turn the flame up brighter, rather than living with a dim flame and turning against myself inside.

You, all of us, we are walking talking firestorms, if we nurture ourselves to be that way.

Potential Blocks

If a person is blocked in the root centre but has a ton of core energy and creative energy, it restricts the energy flow, it's like throwing water or blowing wind on a fire.

There is not a powerful enough flow of energy for it to surge upwards because C1 is calling it back down. It's like a firework that shoots up one foot high and then falls down back to the earth. That's why disappointment can be hard to take or can linger for so long because the energy is getting stuck and isn't releasing.

The root is pulling the energy back into the activities that allow it to feel safe and secure. The physical need for preservation is taking priority. This is why it used to feel like I was constantly stuck in fight or flight mode and under pressure. It's because I was living in a state of physical danger through the root centre.

I walked through life with my jaw locked and shoulders tensed, basing my actions on the avoidance of losing something rather than moving towards what I wanted. I was doing all of this without even knowing it.

Check right now. Is your jaw tenser than it needs to be? Is your body holding any tension in your shoulders or eyebrow? Is your mind racing to avoid the risk of losing time, or losing anything? Smile, breathe out.

See if you can slow down, observe and relax a little more before you continue…. Learning how to restart my energy devices throughout the day has changed the game for me.

* * *

Scarcity is a silent killer of life, in the deluded clothing of righteousness and assertiveness. The stomach tenses because it thinks it's being right, but it's really trying to avoid "looking weak" or incompetent. It's like when a boxer braces their stomach for a punch.

I've put up walls without even knowing myself sometimes. A tense body makes it easy to be irritated, that's why I place importance on mastering my body to release tension and encourage lifeforce flow–otherwise it starts creating problems in my life.

* * *

I remember this one time that I was interviewing for a job. I had the usual week-long, day-long, and hour-before jitters… the usual stuff. I walked into the interview and shook the person's hand with my sweaty palm. We sat down in this bright and intimidating room, which only made it worse.

He asked me how my journey was, and I was not relaxed enough to give him an honest answer. We continued the interview and I answered every question with a sweaty face, beyond nervousness, with my body in fight or flight (default mode for past me). Finally, the guy said, "Hey, how about we talk about what you like to do for fun instead? Let's pause the work stuff for a bit."

We began talking about travel and fitness, the things I loved. I entered into a whole new way of being, switched on and leading the conversation with confidence. My body knew that it was safe because this man was no longer threatening, and we were connecting on a soul level.

The safety system was overridden, my confident fire switched on and burned the fears instantly, and the rest of the interview went fantastic. The guy saw my fire and my potential, so he hired me.

My example points towards why people can be so inspired and energised, but then when it comes to actually unleashing what's inside, we freak out. It's because the safety program is saying "No no no, this is hard. This isn't a good idea, you have to stay here where it's easy and comfortable."

A lot of people tell me that they get knots in their stomachs in certain situations. A pharmaceutical pill isn't the solution. This often has to do with the energy pipe tensing up and holding the energy down there, rather than letting it flow through the body. It's like having one of those water dams with walls up.

Most of the time this happens unconsciously, but it can also happen consciously. You may read a self-help book that sparks insights and you feel ready to change your life, but then nothing changes because your core is not firing powerfully enough for you to go ahead and act on it.

This happened to me for years; I wanted to be a personal trainer for the longest time. I watched others and grew bitter because they were doing what I wanted to do. But I was not willing enough to take the required action to get certified and start a business.

You might even pay for a course, buy a book, or hire a professional (like me), but you could be internally blocking off your own potential by guarding the things you want to be free from.

I've had this ego guard on myself many times and I've lovingly seen this with clients too. It's harder for them to transform when they are so attached to their current way of thinking, or what they "know" is true or will happen.

The core will do whatever it can to create a wall of protection to an identity and what it currently knows, so new stuff will struggle to get in. Neuroscientists have studied this and they say that there is a whole chemical response occurring that pushes out the new and guards the old.

If I know someone is blocked I will do a lot of work with them on relaxing their operating model before trying to help them to see a new inner perspective. As Wayne Dyer says, "Change the way you see the world, and your world changes". I will add to that and say change your energy, and then you can change the way you see your world.

Inner Action and Outer Action

I will often guide my clients into switching on their natural solar fire so they can burn through the illusions of the mind (inner action), both in the short term and long term. I will also push them to take the required outer actions to get to where they want, even if their mind and body resist.

Once they relax a little, they might say "I hate you Raj", in a playful tone and a smiley face. To me, that is a good sign, a little scary is good. Action can create newfound wisdom, a wisdom that provides alternative evidence to the mental noise that it is used to.

That's what I mean by practicing both kriya yoga (internal action) and karma yoga (external action). We can transform our lives by combining both types of action; internal experience and external experience.

Confidence building through action provides real-life proof, rather than trying to massage psychological beliefs. In the past, I have convinced myself that I cannot take outer action until I work through my inner blocks, but I have found that it's not always true.

It's like the classic example of going for a run in the morning, even when our feelings are saying no. Action and willingness get us through that block and we show up, even if we only wake up five minutes into the run.

The block is coming from the mind trying to protect its feelings, to provide an excuse and a roadblock. The term I've used so far to describe this part of ourselves is called ego.

Stepping into the energetic capability of our power centre system is way more potent than trying to reprogram the ego mind. I would go so far as to say that I don't need to try to reprogram it. I can only accept it for what it is–a protection machine.

What I can do is create anew. Create new pathways, ways of operating, ways to function, and enhance my energy flow each day. That is a present-moment experience, and all we have is the present. Future is a present-moment version of me, which results from my present-moment actions.

The Upflow Of Energy

Once you move through these blocks and have a strong core, plus creative energy and feeling grounded, imagine what's possible from here.

This is where it becomes really exciting because Shakti's (your power) flow of energy can start driving upwards in a more powerful way. There is increased energy efficiency, and she has the power of the core to boost her upwards.

The car is fueled up and roaring inside, its engine is powerful and is primed and ready to go to its next destination.

I call this centre the launch pad because this launch pad allows Shakti to surge beyond the lower centres and ascend into the area of the heart. The core centre is where we begin to go from animal into a higher intelligent being.

If you read the book "Sapiens" by Yuval Noah Harari, he states that humans evolved in intelligence when we were able to stand up and allow for an upward energy flow.

Now I don't know if this book is true as "fact-based" truth, but it seems to corroborate with my experience of working with energy flow through my body, as well as the yogic scientific texts.

Scientists say that we evolved from the ground level of all fours and our chest elevated and spine erect so we could angle ourselves in a straight line from the ground to the sky.

This allowed for more energy to flow from the ground toward our brains, allowing us to take in more energy from above. This combination seemed to have evolved us into intelligent beings.

It makes sense, doesn't it? Dr. Joe Dispensa has run various studies that speak of the same, his may sound all sciency, but he's taken the wisdom of the east and turned it into logical western science. He's talking about human evolution through the ancient chakra system.

This is exactly what I am talking about in this book, the tree growing roots and then launching into the sky, that's us. That's what my experience of this energy system has been about–evolving to my maximum capability by evolving in my intelligence of how to navigate this vital force within me.

I realised that we did not stop evolving, I did not need to keep the old patterns that I took through childhood or from watching others. I could learn and grow, just like when I learned that I could mould my body after my first few months in the gym. It was invigorating to see that I could evolve in every area of life by learning how to unleash lifeforce through my power centres.

* * *

Using the launch pad of the core centre is where the magic begins to unfold and we can go beyond personal identity, beyond the physical and mental. The identity of who we are is stored in the core centre, that's why you might experience digestion issues out of the blue, not always because of the food you ate, but sometimes because of a resistance in the mind and its idea of who you are.

I had tons of stomach problems throughout my life. No matter what diet or cleanse I did, it would always come back. The only way that I have found to clear these issues was by working on the finer layers of myself, not just the physical one.

Don't get me wrong, I eat well all year round, and it's pivotal to me to have clear energy flow, but I do not believe that nutrition *alone* will help resolve deeper challenges, it has to be a unified project. They say that a lot of dis-ease starts from the mind; I can vouch for that, and it helped me see how to work with the body and mind as one.

Bringing them into unity is what's really helped, rather than working in silos.

To Summarise

The launch pad of the core centre is the grounding that moves the fire for confident and purified self-expression to be released out of C5 (which we will get onto). The core is the source of personal power, strength, and confidence. Think of it as the system which transforms energy into a usable source. Like exchanging money for goods. Like eating pasta in preparation for a run.

You may or may not be seeing how this tree-like structure is forming. The core forms a part of the trunk of the tree, and we started our journey at the roots. If you know me, you will know that I love trees, they are such a beautiful representation of many aspects of life. We forget, however, that we are built the same way as a tree.

Take a minute now and look back at Maslow's hierarchy of needs and you will see how we are progressing through to higher dimensions of living.

Before we proceed to the heart, I think it would be useful to summarise what the lower centres are all about as a collective unit.

They form a trio, and understanding this trio is important because it will not only help you understand each power centre individually and collectively, but it will also help you relate these centres with how you are living life, as well as how you *can* live life. That's what we will do in the next chapter.

✏️ Questions to consider:

How are you getting into your power to feel strong inside?

What takes you away from this power?

What does strength mean to you? Inside and out.

How is food fueling you and how is it taking away from you? Do an audit of both.

What insights did you take away from this chapter?

What are you excited to learn more about?

The Lower Centres - The Power In Me

*"It is better to conquer yourself than to win a thousand battles.
Then the victory is yours. It cannot be taken from you,
not by angels or by demons, heaven or hell."*
~ Buddha Gautama

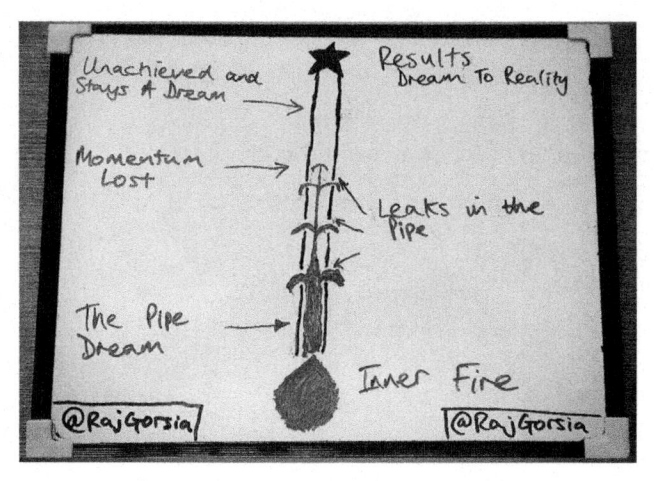

You could say that the first three centres represent our relationship with the body, energy flow and will power. Our needs for survival, creation, and self-empowerment. You can also say that they represent the dynamic nature of humans. The oomphf of the car.

It's the invigorating power that moves through the car. It's the body of the car, the fuel system, and the engine. They thrust the earthly powers through our bodies.

I would say that the lower three centres are where most humans drive their operations from. I know I did, my mind got cloudy because I didn't have much awareness of what was going on in my body.

Stored tension and stagnant energy often occur around these lower centres because the outside world is heavily stimulating them. It definitely was for me; I was stomping around in this clunky body of mine trying to be someone in the world whilst not being fully myself.

These three centres are like the first layers of the onion, the foundational system to ensure we are going to function fine as human beings: like Maslow's pyramid, but different.

Often called the lower triangle, when balanced, they provide a powerful base for our pyramid, allowing for a potent upflow of energy and enabling us to sit with a certain level of peace and vitality.

When these three centres are imbalanced, a ton of digestion challenges, power struggles and scarcity driven decisions can occur. The energy is being focused on trying to fulfill a physiological or psychological need rather than the power centre being used in more intelligent ways.

There's nothing wrong with that, there is no wrong in how we are designed, rather we must learn how to be able to use parts of ourselves better, rather than shunning any one part. Shunning parts is where a lot of my problems resided. Shame and resentment that stayed stuck, me against me, me judging me. That's not very fun to live in now, is it?

The challenge I had was that I had a ton of physical power and ego from the third centre, but low creativity and a massive portion of scarcity soup from the other centres. I was sipping on that soup day and night.

So you can think of it as having some missing links on a railway road, and the train keeps derailing. The energy was leaking into the ground every time I filled it up, like some kind of prank cup.

Mastering the lower three centres can create great success, enjoyment, and a healthy life. Their development is essential, but only focusing on them means true freedom is missing. The fruit of life is missed, and the bark is being drained so much that the wonderful leaves of a person are not glowing and growing the flowers that are beautifully destined to bloom.

Both strong roots and beautiful fruits create the tree of life. And both a strong base and a high top make a powerful pyramid.

I will show you in the next chapters.

✏️ Questions to consider:

How strong would you say your lower trio is, based off what you've read so far?

What are your best ways to ground yourself, to feel your creative juice and feel empowered?

Who are you? Try to answer this question with as much wisdom as you can. First you can answer on the identity you have of your "Self", and then try to answer it by discovering the level beyond that. Keep asking yourself "Who am I?" until you run out of answers.

C4 - The Connection Centre — The Power of Me To We

Chakra Name: *Anahata*
Sanskrit Meaning: *Unstruck or Unbeaten*
Location: *Heart*
Elemental Power: *Air*

"Let my soul smile through my heart and my heart smile through my eyes, that I may scatter rich smiles in sad hearts."
~ Paramahansa Yogananda

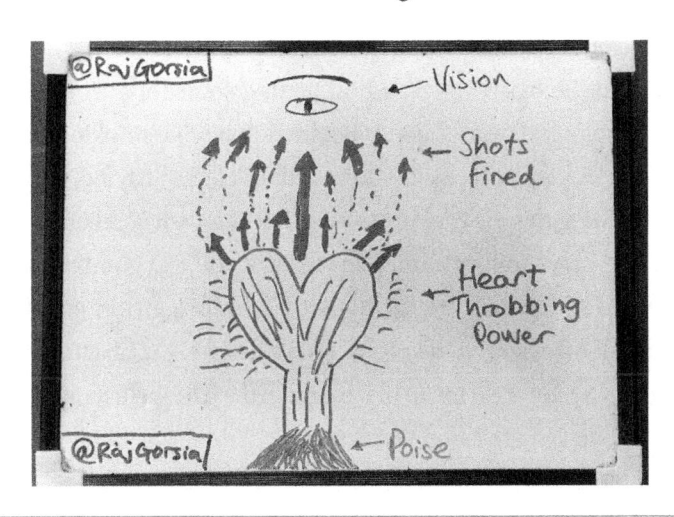

For most of my life, I had seen movies about love. I had heard about this word and concept of love which was thrown around, but I never understood it.

I thought it was something that only existed in movies and wasn't real. I even thought of it as some kind of conspiracy that only women believed in and were trained to want from a man.

My heart was not really activated, heck I would have said that the heart is the cardiovascular organ that I feel when I run, and that's it. I was beyond a pessimist, I shamed those who brought non-tangible topics into a conversation. It felt fluffy and weak.

I have come to learn that most of society doesn't fully understand the heart, just like I didn't. How would I? We cannot be taught love; it has to be something we open up ourselves to experience. It's beyond my logical mind. It can't be put into a smoothie to drink. (Although the well-being industry will keep trying.)

Love is often taken as loving family, partners, or friends. What I have come to understand is that this is only a limited experience of love. True love is boundless, it's the love of everything about life, everything with life, and even things that *seem* life-less, like rocks. Everything around us was created, so how can everything not be seen with the same love if its very creation could only be possible if love was there in the first place?

Love cannot be biased or based on getting something from someone to meet our psychological needs. That is not love, that's like smoking a cigarette to get a hit from it. I chased those hits and they didn't feel satisfying, only satisfying to my fear-avoiding mind. Serving fear only felt like a relief, relief isn't fulfilling.

These days you can hire someone to make you feel good about yourself and make you feel needed and taken care of. I met a girl in Japan who told me that you can hire her for the night, not to do any sexual acts with you but to simply give you an experience of being loved - "the girlfriend experience". (Women hire men in the same way too.)

The problem is that this experience will never really be love, it's a business transaction in order to fill a psychological gap, it's about me me me. The strange thing is that many marriages and relationships are experienced from this place of transaction, the "getting" mentality.

The heart (C4) goes into dormancy when its light is switched off by the illusion of what we think is love but isn't really. I've experienced it many times, I even tried to feel love by having sex with women. It wasn't love, it was a physical and psychological cocktail of pleasure. Love isn't an act of getting pleasure or validation.

Even if you love all things, the truest form of love is not directional or transactional. By that I mean it is not "I love that", or "I love them". It isn't me trying to get love and it isn't love being given either. Love isn't one way. True love is the ability to share one's energy with an energy outside of oneself. It's the connection to this tree, this planet, this sound, this wind, this human, this universe…and the parts of my perceived "self".

Ultimately, the "me" dissolves and a "we" emerges. There is no separation.

It's why a person who truly experiences love does not have strong judgments nor opinions about right or wrong, they are not trying to prove themselves versus another, and they do not feel the need to have one over another or feel lower than another.

Love doesn't live in these states, psychology does. That is why psychologists will send you down a spiral of archetypes and personality types; they are using their psychological mind to separate everything into pieces, into diagnoses and intellectual conclusions.

That is the mind's work, not the hearts. A mind can separate things into a box, but a heart cannot, because the heart is the freedom from the box. A heart can only connect, accept, and care for everything.

It's mind-boggling for me to explain with language but I hope you intuit what I am saying rather than just thinking about it. "mind" boggling is great. The mind does not need to intellectually understand everything to feel it. If you've ever driven a car, you'll find that you feel it, you don't think it. It's an inner experience versus a man-made theory.

I was in the mode of the intellect for my whole life, which is why I never understood love. I had to uncover the wisdom of my heart before I could show others the direction towards finding it for themselves. I am talking from experience with the intention of guiding you toward your own experience and helping you see where to go next.

Unfortunately, there's a lot of complexity where complexity is not needed in the current age of personal development. It's easy for us to get lost in the haze, I know I've gotten lost. I spent years searching, but I did not know what I was searching for or how to find it.

Imagine being in a desert with no idea where you want to even go. Feeling lonely with no idea what to do, only knowing that you feel discomfort. Despite this, I never stopped walking through the desert because I had hope that I would find something, and eventually, I did.

Though I am getting a little ahead of myself because although the heart centre can give you this experience of oneness, true oneness requires the power of the higher centres for the process to fully cultivate.

The heart alone is not the true experience of life, but the heart is the central pillar, the amplifier, the bridge, and the conductor. To me it feels like the key, that's the only way I can describe it. It's the key and central pillar to the full expression of life, because without it, the meeting of Shakti and Shiva (lower world and the upper world) would not be possible.

If the two worlds don't have a bridge, then the fire will blaze inside us with rage. Imagine driving across the country to see your partner and as you approach a bridge (the heart), it begins to close. Imagine you are told by the government that you cannot go any further and you must turn back.

Imagine the frustration? "I can't go? I won't see my other half?!" RAGE!

The rage occurs as a result of the energy being sent downwards so the lower centres begin to get overloaded and overheat. You know how it goes, too much air conditioning and your throat hurts, too much sun and you get burnt. Too much of something often creates a problem in any electrical system, and we too have an electrical system.

The flow of energy wants to rise, the dynamic force in you wants to meet the heavens and turn into illuminating peace, like a firework.

Shakti will burn you if she is blocked off at C4, and this can manifest as experiences of sadness, anger, and depression among others if you don't let her pass. Remember, Shakti isn't a female, and Shiva isn't a male. They are two of the same, two sides to a coin. Dynamic power is Shakti and still awareness is Shiva. Yin and yang.

Think of three examples right now where you've felt this experience that I have just described. This is also a chance for you to use what you've gathered from the book up to this point.

* * *

Baby You're a Firework

Being in the way creates a lot of turmoil. It isn't a bad thing, and it isn't a problem, and we don't really do it consciously, but this is what's happening. It's happened to me throughout my life and I still face it from time to time.

This is why I suffered from inner challenges, not because I had a "disorder", but because I was suppressing the life in me that demanded to express itself up and out of me.

Like a firework, its only destiny is to soar and burst into a beautiful illumination, and then fall to the ground and die peacefully. The firework is gone, its purpose is met. That's our purpose too, to be fully lit up in our lives and then go back to the nothingness we came from, peacefully.

It may be why Hinduism talks about reincarnation because the firework didn't quite light up the sky, so it has to come back over and over again until it does. Imagine how this process must feel. "Ah, not again… okay let's keep trying!"

No wonder there's sometimes frustration. It's like being aroused by a partner into experiencing a ton of energy but not liberating it. Unfulfilled Shakti power can create similar feelings to this, but in continuous everyday scenarios.

This connection of Shiva and Shakti resonates with me on a humanistic level more than the concept of yin and yang, because it teaches me that the true reason why these polarities exist together rather than separately is that they represent the uniting journey of love between two entities. Two who are ultimately one. It's beautiful.

As I said earlier, there is no such thing as male or female genders on an energy level, so remember that this is beyond physical genders, it's about our two powers as humans. I only use "she", and "he" as a way to help you create a story to describe what is going on inside.

Who doesn't love a story? That's why Eastern wisdom is so enchanting, it's full of stories. This isn't for fun, there is an intelligence behind it, they knew that stories were a way for us to go beyond the psychological and intellectual mind and access more profound wisdom. Zen Koans are also a great example of this. So are Sufi poems.

As a homework, check some Koans and Poems out on Google and see what it does to you. For me, I am stunned into silence, it does something that logic cannot do. They are designed that way.

Common Sense Wisdom

To me, life is about uniting entities (like people, skills, tools, energies, and anything else) through the glue of love. And yes, I'm quite the romantic if you are wondering. It only happened when I began releasing and expressing the power from my heart.

We can go into common sense and science and simply look at the location of the heart. It is centrally placed for a reason rather than out of coincidence, it's there because it's the bridge fusing the upper and lower worlds together, both physically and subtly. It's literally the central point of our being.

This type of common sense never occurred to me in the past. It only occurred to me once I was experiencing a higher level of consciousness, with my logical/conditioned mind out of the way.

Like eating a pineapple for the first time, when you experience it then you know it. Reading about the taste of pineapple on Google will never give you direct wisdom about its taste.

So my invitation to you is to be open with this entire piece of writing. I don't know if it will shine insight onto everyone, or whether it can be verified by modern science. I know that true intelligence, like eating the apple, has to be taken in from an angle that is not purely intellectual science, it has to be an experimental and intuitive science.

Ancient Indian sciences and other traditions have proven measurements between planets thousands of years ago. They learned it through intuitive intelligence, just as I've been pointing you towards.

I was walking around Machu Pichu in Peru and I wondered how on earth the Incan empire had access to such an incredible level of intelligence. I asked the guide and he said that they used the wind, the sun, the sea levels, and the herbs in nature to tune into an elevated intelligence. They then passed down teachings to each other, practically, not theoretically.

When Albert Einstein spoke about the theory of relativity, he said:

> "It occurred to me by intuition, and music was the driving force behind that intuition. My discovery was the result of musical perception."

He took long baths so he could get out of his head and tap into intuition. Every part of his genius he credited to intuition. In the quote he says music was the driving force behind that intuition, and I believe he is talking about the flow of lifeforce moving through his being. The musical ear which can listen out for more than the intellectual voice, it can hear something beyond the self.

When we can go beyond the self, we tap into everything else. And what is there beyond the personal? There is the impersonal. And if it is impersonal to me, and to everyone, then whose is it? Nobody's right? It's universal. It's everyone's.

Tapping into the "everyone mode" takes us from me to we. From my experience, that is what has taken me out of judging others, comparison and any disconnect between me and others, me and life.

C4 (the heart) is a relationship creator, it's what makes things sweet and makes me smile at someone else, melting inside as I do so. It's the grand connector and amplifier of aliveness.

Practice this–The next person that you see, smile at them with a loving knowing that you are one. See how it goes, really try your best.

This isn't to show you that I am right about what I wrote, it's to get you to test out what I wrote after you take it in, even if "you already know" this stuff. What harm can it do to let me in and play with things that I am saying to you?

My Summary of C4

C4 is the power centre that amplifies all other centres. It removes fears and doubts, it is like throwing the sweetness into the recipe of our existence because it turns the focus from me to we. It does this energetically rather than through mental force (which hardly ever helps, I've tried.)

When you feel compassion for another human, when you are enjoying nature, when you feel sad, when you feel blissful, when you are "out of the head" as we say — it's your heart that is lighting up inside.

Without this sensation of connection to something more than the walls of "me me me me me", what would we be? Love is the original language, and it is the glue that bonds things together, not just for us as humans, but it's doing this with the entire universe.

When it rains outside, what tells the plant that rain and itself have a connection? What mechanism tells the plant that water is something it has within itself and is okay to let in and feel? It's love. Love is the transmitter, the barrier breaker, the connecting fluid, the glue.

* * *

We spend time going on vacations because we seek connection, we have relationships because we seek connection. We are angry and sad when we feel isolated and our survival response kicks in, disconnection. Disconnection from everything, and focused on me being secure, psychologically, and physiologically.

When I pushed ex-girlfriends away and blamed them for something, it was a defense mechanism, I became a wolf who felt threatened. Not by them, but by my fear of danger. I put myself into an aggressive state to try to stay safe. I can love myself for seeing this, rather than shaming myself. I am human, *and* I can be wiser than that, not just accept it as default or using it as a victim statement.

I have heard people use their humanness as a victim statement. "It's my defense system". Okay, now what? Are you going to sit there stuck in that feeling of "brokenness" forever? We aren't helpless children anymore and we definitely aren't broken.

We have a choice to be wiser, to be beyond the mind and body's program or previous karma. This is what I tell you because I discovered it for myself by using my heart to help me transcend into a smarter way of operating. It helped me to free myself from so much tension.

The heart allows for a more powerful expression of us and it's how we know that we are more alive than robots. The Tin Man in the movie Wizard of Oz, Pinocchio, and every other related movie are speaking to us so powerfully because they are expressing the desire to feel whole and fully alive. Pinocchio says "I'm a real boy!" He is so awe-struck because of the feeling of aliveness running through him.

That's exactly how I felt when I began awakening parts of myself that I had locked away inside my C4. I had so much tension inside my heart and entire system that the more I looked into it, the more I saw that I did not see myself "as a real boy". Meaning, I saw myself as broken.

I saw myself as disconnected and isolated. When I began flooding the heart gates open, it washed away the illusion that I had been living in most of my life. The things I was doing to try to feel alive and connected (like watching porn) were flawed as a system.

Look at yourself with great attention, what are the kinds of things you are doing to try to feel alive, whole, or to feel love? Make a list right now.

And while you are doing that, make a list of which of those actually help take you there, versus which give you the illusion of it.

You can arrange the list in one column, two columns, or however your creativity flows. Make it a homework exercise that you spend five minutes on.

Potential Blocks

Here's the thing, when our C4 is being blocked off by our psychological mind programs, love can disguise itself as a muddy version of itself. Muddied by the insecurities, fears, and resentment from our past.

I remember being in art class as a kid and the naughty kid (not me!) would put black paint into everyone's paint pots because it seemed fun to him. The sky blues, the grass greens and rosy reds would quickly fade into darkness. The color went and there was a murky black liquid left. That is what the mind can do, dilute the colour inside us into dark clouds, until we can't see any colour.

When I was traveling with a girl in Peru, I often experienced times when I was worn out and got irritated very easily. One of these times we were in the Taj Mahal together. Imagine, being in one of the greatest sights in the world, but a polluted mind to spoil the experience.

I complained about the crowd, I complained about the heat, I complained about her wanting to take so many photos, I argued with people trying to sell me something, I ruined the only time she and I would probably ever visit this place.

She bought an Indian sari and wore the full Bollywood outfit, she was from the other side of the world in Latin America so being in India and looking like a Bollywood star was a childhood dream of hers. They don't get saris where she lives, she only saw them on TV and wished she could wear one.

I mixed my black paint of me me me into her colours, and as much as her natural positive vibe tried to lift me up, it couldn't. Finally, she burst into tears and said, "You've ruined my dream, Raj, I've been dreaming about this for my entire life, and you've spoiled it!"

It hit me. She woke me up with a shot of lifeforce, and I felt my heart swell up inside as I looked at this beautiful woman dressed up in her lovely outfit, an outfit from my own heritage that she was proudly wearing.

What the hell had I done? She cried for two hours in bed. I sat there next to her and she said. "Raj, your eyes just go black and you see the whole world as against you. I always try to help you see the light but sometimes it's too powerful, I can't say anything that will stop you."

These black eye moments have followed me around for my entire life, I have tears in my eyes as I write this. I really questioned who I was being from that day onwards. We only had two days left together before we flew to separate sides of the world, and I held such deep shame and guilt that continued with me even after we said goodbye.

That shame eventually turned into the type of pain which propelled me and propels all of us humans into changing something forever. From that point onward our relationship improved because I vowed to watch out for any moment that my mind wished to put black paint into the colors, and I'd commit to not letting myself do it again.

That insight stuck with me forever. No matter where we are in the world, no matter how beautiful it looks on the outside, we can still ruin an experience if we throw dark paint all over it.

The Power Centres

My initial face, no smile. A moody git as we say in the UK.

The smile of freedom after I woke up to how much of a moody git I was being. This was at the end of the day though, so she had spent hours with a tense version of me. This smile was my attempt to clear the black paint that I had thrown all over the place.

Raising The Flow Higher

I think that we are different from animals because we have a higher level of consciousness and can analyse ourselves. The analysis often creates so many assumptions which affect our being state. Animals can also feel emotions, but they don't spend time analysing their past or crying over a fantasy future worry.

Humans tend to do this because we have the ability to use our minds to direct our creative energy, survival energy, and our desire for empowerment as a way of blocking us instead of freeing us.

When the energy is focused on creating fires in the lower centres, then the energy doesn't even see that it can explore further by rising and spreading itself in a balanced way across the higher centres.

If it doesn't see this as a possibility, then it isn't its fault, it's doing its best job. It's up to us to improve the flow, it's up to us to raise our consciousness, to see what is happening in here, and to get out of the way and nurture the lifeforce energy so it can move. Shakti wants to move.

David R. Hawkins has written a prolific book called "letting go". This book explains the energy system in a slightly more scientific way, it may help you digest what I am saying in this book. In essence when he says, "let go", I translate it to, let it flow, let it move. Michael Singer has also written some great books about this. He's a modern-day yogi like me, so I like his style.

Getting Your Centres In a Twist

To add to what I just said, think about it like this...

If the third centre of the core is tied in knots, then the heart may be quietened by the ego and judgments. It may prioritise personal power over love. Personal power is great, but not when it's led by imbalances from the other power centres such as worry that "people are dangerous" or "I am not good enough" or "expressing my energy is shameful".

This is how it was for me; I was a big strong man who believed I had to be someone in the world but at the same time I had insecurities about being someone in the world. I was at war with myself. One side is saying "Go for it!" while the other side is saying, "Don't go!"

The same thing happened when I wanted to connect with someone. My heart wanted it, but another part of me was scared of wanting it, blocking off the connection so nobody could feel the warmth of my heart. Then again, wanting it, and playing little games to get a taste of it, but then holding back on having the full extent of the connection. It was draining and confusing as hell.

They call it "falling in love" for a reason, because we have to let go, we cannot be half in half out when we fall.

It's like a tug of war without the relief of having a winner. Even if you lose a tug of war, at least you can go home and forget about it. The inner tug of war was way more tiring for me, holding on for too long and getting rope burn.

One example that highlights this was when I wanted to write a book, it has always been a life goal of mine to write a book. I felt empowered and creative enough to go for it, but the safety response kicks in and says, "Who am I to write about life in such a deep way?!", "What if it's not good enough?", "What if someone shames me and tells me that I am wrong?"

They call it "imposter syndrome", or you may call it "freaking out".

Notice how personal those questions are? They are identity-threatening, so the root centre (C1) which is related to the physical body creates a physical sense of danger inside me. The core centre (C3) related to my identity feels insecure, and the creative flow (C2) restricts the release of energy into my body, and the hose pipe gets squeezed into a knot. Everything I do turns into a weaker version of me, less poised, less potent.

The body fires up and creates adrenaline, the life-loving closes off at the heart and the whole system calls in more emergency recruits to stop this body from taking action in writing the book. "No writing for you Raj, that's dangerous, you could die!" As dramatic as it sounds, that is the neurological process that happens inside of us which kills our flow and discourages us. Sound familiar?

The only way out of that is to show the physical body it is safe by having a realisation that writing the book is not dangerous. And to nurture myself, use love versus fear, connection versus disconnection, which means turning on a light and a lightness.

That's why I put a huge focus on the body and its vitality in how I live and how I support others, the body has to be treated well.

It's also why I only intend to write for an hour at a time. If I think about writing for more than an hour then my mind might say "that's too much effort, why do it?"

If I naturally write for longer than an hour, I will. If I decide beforehand then there is a chance that my mind will block me off and procrastinate. I love putting a timer next to me too because now the whole thing becomes a game and has some structure. When I work with my clients I talk a lot about gamifying life and playing, because it loosens us up.

Hearty Fuel

Here's another example, we may express our creative energy and feel a connection to our heart, but an unbalanced core centre might throw us off course. I've felt this when my body was over-exhausted or dealing with inflammation from food that doesn't serve me.

The oomphf, the drive, the fuel system is out of service. I need to master how I use food in order to effectively use the power inside me. The core is a battery pack of potential, and if I mess around with it and put junk into the system or don't care for it then it has to spend fuel cleaning up that mess rather than helping me do what I want to do.

For example, if I have cow's milk then I notice a response inside my body that is lethargic and slow. I don't have anything against cows; I am not an environmentalist; I am a scientist. I run an experiment and see a result, over continuous testing periods.

So I now know, don't drink milk and you win. The same with processed foods and caffeine, sugar, and other junk. I got a zero policy. But if I mess up once in a blue moon, I don't beat myself up over it, I forgive myself. Meal timing and the amount of food also comes into play, because if I am eating too much or too often then my body will go into an inflamed state.

I used to abuse my stomach, I was eating when I *thought* I was hungry, versus seeing food as a tool to help fuel my state of being and fuel the efficiency of my actions. Eating isn't a pleasure-focused activity in my eyes; pleasure can be a byproduct, but the priority is having a clear energy flow that can be used for inner peace and outer expression.

But before I get too deep into that, I want to also say that the core doesn't just relate to food, there's a lot more going on in there. It's the control room of the Self. The identity, the fuel and mover of us. So even a thought or spoken words can create the same reaction that the milk does.

Do you see how intricately connected this system is? This is why I say that we cannot have a logic-driven process, we cannot see these centres as separate entities. Our use of this system must be a dance between each of these inner forces and their relation to the outside world. That's why I speak about unification so much.

* * *

The Amplifier Effect

Once we allow ourselves to experience elevated emotions from the heart, we allow Shakti to continue her journey toward her destiny, her partner, Shiva… she's getting closer.

Once C4 is truly open, the ride becomes way easier because the heart turns into a powerful amplifier. It took me many years of living with a closed heart to learn everything I have mentioned here.

My heart was so closed that I never felt emotion for anyone, I was so focused on "fixing" and "firefighting" the surface-level challenges I faced that I never once considered the heart as a useful (and powerful) mode of being.

The old me would have said, "I haven't got time for that fluffy heart stuff Raj! I have real challenges to deal with". I would have literally shot down any idea about an inner world and most of this book would have gone over my head.

But once I did begin to focus my heart, running energetic experiments with it, it opened me up massively and allowed me to take leadership over the feelings of tension and insecurity that I had. It allowed me to activate the goodness in all the power centres and helped me to switch on all the lights. That's what the heart can do, and why it's the central pillar.

It's like the game Pac-Man, when you eat the special circle (activate C4), the monsters inside the maze turn another colour. You go from running away to being powerful, and you can eat the monsters up and gain points from them.

That's what I love to do, eat every discomfort, eat every pain, eat it all up and use it for learning, not to get egotistical and barbaric about it, but rather simply, calmly, eat everything up and use it for fuel. That's what a yogi does, use every single resource, every occurrence, everything, for goodness and learning, wasting nothing.

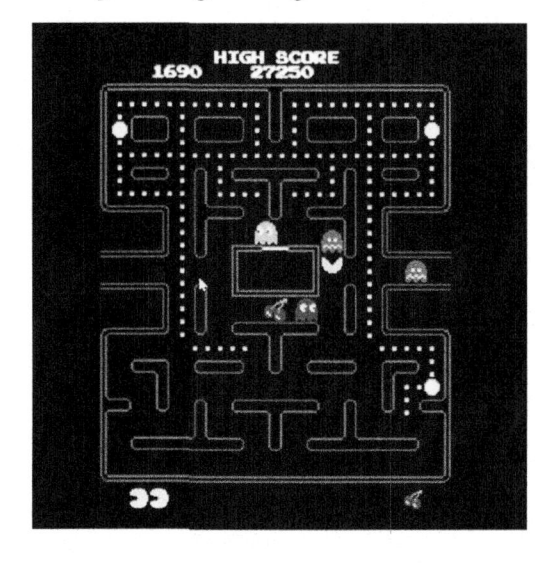

Love is like one of those scents that fill the entire room with its essence. Even if you have smelly socks coming from your mind, the heart will amplify your state so high that its scent can overpower the other smells, to a point that they transform into the same lovely scent.

Love turns everything into beauty. I'd be sitting there euphorically smiling at plants, like I was on drugs. No matter how cold or dark it is outside, we can be colorful and warm inside.

To End - Next Stop...

After this opening of the heart occurred, I found myself wanting to connect with more people, being more compassionate with people and wanting to help them by talking about my journey, hence I'm here.

I even created a business through it where I am magnetically attracting the people who want my help in unleashing their superpowers. I can only do this if I am really loving them into being their best. There is no other way, the heart must be involved.

I am like Professor X in the X-Men, helping people who feel like mutants to find their way, feel supported, and unlock their powers to amplify their experience of life to the best it can be.

When grounded in the lower centres and powerfully open in the heart (or you could say being super Pac-Man), I felt like sharing the love, giving it to everyone else like a piece of cake.

Cake is way better shared than alone, right? That's why I have been using my voice and my energy to help others, which leads us perfectly to the next section... how to raise the energy from within and burst it out into the world like cannons of light.

This happens through the next power centre, C5, the expression centre. I call it the roarer. Roaring the music box of pure truth from inside of us.

✏ Questions to consider:

This has been a lovely chapter for me to write. What did it spark in you? Really slow this one down.

When have you felt wholesome, full of light, and full of heart? Write down a few examples. Most people forget about who they've been because they are too focused on what's next.

When have you felt closed in your C4? Write down some examples.

When have you felt the interconnected challenges going on in the lower centres and the heart? E.g. you energetically wanted to speak to that person about a topic, but you felt insecure. Or you felt connected to an idea but did not feel empowered enough to act on it. Think of your own examples and write them down. What wants to happen?

What aren't you seeing yet? It's useful to know what we cannot see, without scarcity, but with curiosity.

Please take some time to reflect on everything you've read so far before proceeding. Even 15 minutes will be useful.

If you get the first four centres moving powerfully in sync, your life experience will massively amplify. I know it did for me.

They are the first 4 wheels of your car. So reflect on the ride and cruise for a bit, before we look at the next 3 wheels.

C5 - The Expression Centre - The Power To Be A Roarer

Chakra Name: *Vishuddi*
Sanskrit Meaning: *Purity*
Location: *Throat*
Elemental Power: *Space*

"Speak with integrity. Say only what you mean. Avoid using the word to speak against yourself or to gossip about others. Use the power of your word in the direction of truth and love."
~ Don Miguel Ruiz

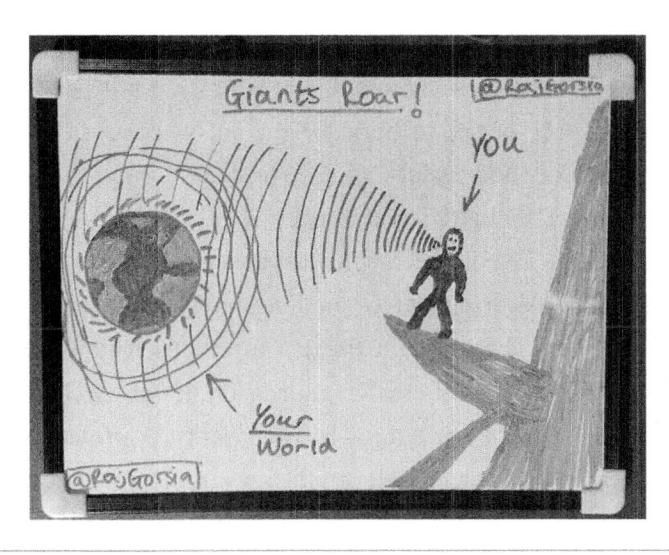

As I continued upwards on this journey through my energies, I began to experience a pure bursting of aliveness. I began riding the creative force like one of those rodeo bulls, moving with it rather than fighting it, and I felt something inside me that yearned to be expressed. I realised that once the heart is filled with lifeforce power, we begin to generate a super cannon of energy that collects in the throat like a lake collecting water.

This elixir of energy is like a cannon of light that contains all the powers from all the other centres combined, and it can be fired anywhere that we want. Like having our own version of the sun coming out from our mouths, warming, and bringing light to the world.

C5 holds the potential to outwardly express what is inside of us in an authentic way. The level of strength of this superpower depends upon the level of potency, space, and purity that we have awakened and cultivated within us.

The way I began to (and still) feel this within myself was like having a waterfall of energising light that is ready to roar out of my mouth, and I can release it in different shapes to hit every single person who comes into contact with it. I have learned that "I", meaning my personal ideas of who I am, must not get in its way or try to contain it.

I am clear in knowing that a lot of my challenges throughout life revolved around not expressing myself, not letting out this light. It hurt me so bad that my face began to burst bright red whenever I was holding something in and my body went into fight or flight. I thought I had a social anxiety problem, I thought I was broken, but it turned out I was just blocking off the volcano of light, so the inside began to burn.

It's like building yourself up to something and then getting in your head, so it doesn't happen. The voice, the throat, our actions, it all works the same way as this natural process of creative expression. If our psychology gets in the way then the flow of our energy becomes jerky. A professional sports player, a singer, or a dancer will tell you the same thing. Hesitate and you go out of "the zone".

* * *

It's at this point in Shakti's rising adventure from C1 to C5 that she (we, our power) is being drawn by the supreme intelligence (Shiva) closer towards it and we can finally feel the allure of what it feels like as we get closer.

This supreme intelligence has been calling for our entire lives whether we knew it or not. If we heard it, we did something about it to get closer to it, whether that was a travel adventure, business building, pleasure activities or anything else to find that ultimate release or fulfillment. We heard it, and in a roundabout way we did whatever we could to get us closer.

We came from one source, and we are always being beckoned toward our fullest potential, before returning back to the source. That is Shiva's calling. He wants us to experience the ultimate expression of ourselves, the grand cycle of fireworks lighting the sky and then falling.

* * *

At this stage of the system, at C5 (the expression centre) we begin to finally have a taste for what it might feel like, the inside expressing out versus trying to get the outside to go in.

Writing this book is an example of this. It feels exciting; I am working through the power of C5, and all of my energies and other centres are sending energy toward it, using the hands, the voice and all of my energy outlets to focus on the activity I am engaged in.

C5 is focused like a hose pipe being pointed at one plant. The plant of this book will get all the life-giving energy at this moment, and later I will point it at something else. Conscious and purified outbursts of my energy, rather than letting it spill all over the place, like a leaky bucket.

* * *

The Superhero's Origin Story

When going into the full expression we feel the energy of a prolific public speaker and a glorious singer, because what else are they doing but expressing their energy in a focused way? A singer will say "Sing with your heart!" and when they do, they hit those high notes that tingle the listener's bodies into wondrous silence, like zombies being stunned into life by light bursting through their bodies.

The very idea of expressing this light creates such a buzz of energy that we will naturally feel the desire to shine it onto everyone. This is exactly how it felt for me; I used to be a closed-off person who kept myself to myself. I looked out for me and only me; well when I began to experience this light, I wanted to use my throat as an instrument to awaken others, like a lion on top of a rock who's waking up the jungle with a roar. It was intrinsic and a calling rather than an extrinsic and psychological search for approval, praise, or a reward.

* * *

Why else would someone see something like the process of writing a book, speaking at events, and leading people as joy vs a means to an end? I do it because I experience such aliveness when I do it, it feels so fulfilling. I didn't choose to do this, I'd happily watch Netflix and sit on the sofa if it felt right, but it doesn't. Something inside me, which is beyond me, wants me to express itself. It tells me, "This is your duty, your purpose, speak, act, go and inspire the world."

Of course, the psychological voice inside me resists, every single time. It doesn't want to be seen, doesn't want to be judged and doesn't want to do anything but preserve itself. That part isn't refreshing and energising though is it? You tell me.

The part of me which is courageous and expresses itself is definitely energising, beyond the psychological drama in my mind and the pulsing anxiety in my body. I was challenged with self-expression for most of my life, but it turns out that I was made for it if I did it in a way that felt like the pure me rather than how I "should be".

I unlocked this ability to communicate from a connected place rather than competitive. I became open about my journey, not wishing to hide anything and getting vulnerable to show the naked me–just as I was born, naked. I found expression so difficult for most of my life because I was trying to avoid looking weak, whilst wanting to look strong.

People often do not believe me when I say that speaking has been my biggest life challenge. I tell them, it isn't the speaking that's hard, it's being free to be myself that was hardest.

I knew what to say, I had a glorious speaker visualised in my head, but when it came down to it, I cracked, I made myself small and I beat myself up about it. It's the deep-rooted fear of judgment and shame that was the blocker to the pure voice coming out of me. As I've said before, we have all the potential inside us, it's the things that restrict the flow that limit us.

It takes me back to childhood memories when I was told "Don't do that", or when I was laughed at, or when I was questioned, "Why aren't you mixing with others", or when I felt so much was wrong with me because I couldn't be "normal" like everyone else. I felt like there was pressure to speak, to be a certain way, and to be different from how I was.

That's how the human experience seems to go for some of us, the sensitive soul of developing little me took the events and turned them into programs of "I am not okay as a human". So I hid away a lot of who I really was, locking it away in a chamber inside my heart, in exile.

Can you relate to what I've said in a way?

The thing I want to point you towards is to see that we have a perception of the past that may feel like a sad story, but we also have the ability to bring ourselves into present-moment intelligence, to see how we can flip the story. I have found it really useful to shift every moment of the past into a part of my superhero origin story. Like when Peter Parker's grandfather died, he was ignited into becoming Spiderman.

Shrinking Violet

C5 is all about purified communication, it represents being able to release what is inside without adding layers or holding back. Holding back usually happens because of a psychological barrier; it's like throwing a massive rock into a lake that doesn't erode but just sits there and we become accustomed to the modified energy flow that it elicits, and it becomes the "normal".

Have you ever been with a group of people and you've wanted to say something but didn't? That was me. I believed that I had a massive social anxiety issue, but I then realised that social anxiety was only the tip of the iceberg (to my horror). I had real blocks in speaking because my feelings about who I was turned my whole physical body into a war machine, fight or flight.

The worst thing was that I did not ever express myself in a war-like way, I was a shrinking violet. Have you ever heard of the term? It is a beautiful flower that wilts because it does not want to be seen. It collapses, choosing not to proudly show its beauty. That was me, hesitating and keeping it all in. My boss at my first real job told me that I was a shrinking violet after I choked when he asked me to give a speech, that's how I learnt this term.

Every time I have not expressed myself fully it has been because I felt this barrier in my way. I always regretted it afterward and I would judge myself in a discouraging low state. Whether that was talking to girls at school, raising my hand to speak in a group, or taking action on my dreams such as starting a business.

We say, "I am feeling down" and it makes sense anatomically because we send the energy potential back down the shaft and into the ground again. We send it to its death; we kill our own vibration so it makes sense that it would feel "low". It's like shouting at a kid to be quiet when they are being their most expressive self.

No wonder we develop ways to conceal or suppress our energies as adults. But that doesn't mean blaming our upbringing, instead, I am informing you for you to become a creator of your present. Our present determines the future we find ourselves in.

Instead of feeling down, let's get grounded in the present and roar up and out, from the centre of our being.

Release A "Sigh" Out

As I began to look more closely, I noticed that when I have had blocked energy in my C5 it has often resulted in physical pain inside my throat, and congestion in my heart and lungs. It has usually resulted from me not allowing a voice to speak. Whether that voice speaks internally or externally, either way, it wants to be heard.

Internal combustion occurs when I push that voice away and suppress it, telling it to "shut up and be quiet". So it sits inside of me curled up and scared to speak, even speak to myself. It hides because it's been shut down and scared off by another part of me. Isn't that crazy? It makes sense why an internal restriction can be felt. Can you relate?

I discovered that I was pushing away the natural flow of life itself. It's like trying to stop feces from moving out of my anus. Uncomfortable right?

Unleashing the natural life energy from our throat feels like a sigh. Think about the neurological process of a sigh for a moment. And try it right now. Sigh out, get interactive with me.

There is a sound, there is a release, there is energy moving up and out of you right?

Now try the same thing but this time say "ahhhhh" in a high pitch. Notice the vibration moving from your belly through your heart and out of your mouth. It's wonderful isn't it?

If you now try it with full force, holding nothing back, you will understand what I've been saying throughout this chapter.

Ready…. "ahhhhhhhhhhhhh".

Hey, if you didn't do it, don't worry, you did it inside by reading the words. Inside and out both synching is even more liberating though. It must be how Mariah Carey feels when she hits those majestic notes.

We have a delightful musical instrument of energy in our throats. Remember, it isn't just about speaking, it's about how we use our entire bodies to take action. The arms connect to the throat too–so does the mind, and the throat helps to quiet the mind and embody our energy.

The heart also connects to the throat, the heart sits in the middle and allows us to control how sharply and how powerfully we use our bodies to take action and release our expression out of us.

I have had sessions with my clients where they burst into liberating tears because they unleashed a level of expression that they've never let out before. I set them some assignments to get them to use their voice to speak and use their bodies to take actions that they would have struggled with in the past, and their transformation skyrocketed.

The reason why these actions happened is because we planted a foundation seed of power through the body, so it could reveal its petals through the heart and throat. Therefore, taking action outside of the session was easier, because they did it from the seed of empowerment, rather than the isolated mind.

Over time, the seed grows, until the flowers bloom, and they roar a scent of color into the world.

I know that if I can get out what is inside of me out in the world, then I am truly alive. This goes for ideas, dreams, passions, expression of love, speaking confidently, action-taking, and everything else that involves impression into expression.

Why Is This So Exhilarating?

From my experience, it's because it's an experience of the lifeforce itself entering into me and using me as a conduit to express something out into the world. It's bigger than the mind, bigger than me me me me me.

Like giving birth, it's a co-creation with the seed of life, doing the work that life has put into our DNA potential. Women are not "doing" pregnancy, it's occurring through them.

Even famous entrepreneurs have birthed success by using the higher forces that I have described in this book, either unconsciously or consciously. How else would a human create physical success from something that began as just an idea inside them?

C5 had to be involved, as have the other centres. Hear me correctly, the power centres had to be involved, the analytical mind alone could not have done any of it. It isn't possible.

From Inside to Outside, Impression To Expression

Think of it like this: there is a process by which the most intelligent waterfall-like energy can come from inside of us and pour out of the throat. Some people might call that flow.

It's like hitting a drum and hearing a sound. Nothing existed before the drum was hit, but suddenly, bang. That's what a developed C5 does, it produces a natural vibrational impact.

People speak about manifestation, and what they are doing is latching onto the idea of what is possible for us humans if we can really align our energies.

The manifestation thing can be taught in a watered-down way though and become fluffy (as I like to call it). Fluffy, or limp, like one of those limp handshakes or hugs. I want full potency, not a watered-down version.

The manifestation teachings can often only feed the ego, to create a false sense of control that it so desires. So again, we stay stuck in the psychological maze.

From my experience, true manifestation can occur when the power centres are truly in alignment, it cannot just be a mental masturbation of repeating "I am" statements. The whole body has to be lit up and relaxed at the same time and we must enter into an energy of operating that transcends the ego mind.

Why? Because it's so easy for the mind to undermine, or work from ego in spiritual clothing. The system must be aligned so that the outpouring of actions and speech can be drawn from a pure and reliable source.

I once bought some ashwagandha from amazon, and I noticed that it was having adverse effects. It wasn't relaxing me; it was irritating me. I intuitively knew that this wasn't like the well-sourced ashwagandha that I got from India, even if it seemed like it was. The texture was different and so was the effect. It works the same with every source we draw upon in life; it must be reliable, the real deal, top quality, not a weak version.

I know for myself that the highest stance possible in terms of both inner impression and outer expression can occur if my roots are deep, the core lit up, the heart open, and the throat plugged into all of those appliances.

You don't need to call yourself a spiritual person to utilise the potential of the expression centre. Everyone is using it already, it's a basic human faculty. I have spewed out venomous words from my mouth and hurt people's feelings before, and I have taken actions that have not been for my highest good or the world's.

On the other hand, I have used the power of C5 to speak in a rhythm that requires zero planning or thinking, I have sung loving words to people which shines light into their whole being. And more simply, I have been friendly in my tone, facial expressions and energy to the person that I've ordered food with, as simple as that.

I use this centre all day long, and we are all using it. So the thing I learned is that if I can optimise the way it functions and my level of mastery in using it (as a tool), then I can create a life that feels fulfilling, connective and musical, and most importantly, do it all effortlessly.

This power inside us can either create magic or create a mess.

Potential Blocks

If you notice any blocks based on anything I just said then it means that there's probably a clog in the pipe, even if you feel safe, energetic, courageous, or connective through the other power centres.

Have you ever tried to hold yourself from going to the toilet? It's uncomfortable and its tense, because its fate is being stopped by us, we are standing in the way of the pee's destiny.

It has to come out and it will come out, it's up to us whether we hold it in until it comes out as a mess all over us, or we let it out as it's meant to come out–as a pleasant release.

This suppression can cause a huge amount of upset for a person, I know it did for me. I was so busy trying to figure out what was wrong with me inside that I didn't even think that there was something wanting to come out of me.

I became so biased on the inner world–although it was serving me well to do so at the time–that I forgot that living a fully expressed life also creates wisdom, not just looking inward all day long.

Yes, inward is vital, but it can sometimes be masked in a clever illusion in itself, it can become a trap of the ego. That's what I realised I was doing, making more illusions than freedom by some of the types of "inner work" that I got drawn into.

The blocks or smoke of illusion are often connected to the entire system. The fearing mind creates ideas and we get so drawn into them. I had blocks with performance, with speaking about myself, with trusting others and even around my choices of food that went into my mouth.

Instead of seeing myself as broken, I realised that I could work on these things the same way that I would work on a pipe that had blocks. Instead of judging myself or the pipe, I can work with the reality, clearing the smoke of illusion and simply becoming better.

The block must be treated as a holistic investigation, like Sherlock Holmes looking for clues in all places. If someone calls themselves a "throat chakra healer", question them as to what they will really help you with.

If they say that they do some magical ritual on your throat alone, question them some more. Find out how the work they are doing will actually help you in your day-to-day life (not just a temporary buzz). Also find out how deeply they worked on their own life too. The blind leading the blind happens all too often. Learn from people who really know their stuff.

It's easy to get caught in illusions. Some professionals will consciously or unconsciously entangle you into a new illusion, or get you deeper stuck in your own. So my invitation is to direct you toward your inner guru, the same way every outside person's role is to aid you with that same purpose.

Pouring Out A Glorious Roar

At one point I wondered, if I could surpass the blocks in my expression centre, imagine what would be possible.

When I am in my full expression, I am expressing whatever I want from the depths of my being. No need to think what to say, no need to suppress or hold back. It's a no-mind approach and a pouring out like a lion's roar. Imagine a lion's roar which was half-baked? It wouldn't wake up the jungle. They'd stay asleep.

Like a waterfall, it keeps on giving but it flows gracefully without any effort. The water's natural path is to go down, and our energy's natural path is to come in, move through us, go up and burst out like a light show.

It's like when actors improvise; they are operating from flow, there is no thinking. It's full liberation because the energy inside takes over and does the work. Some call it "flow *state*", but from my experience, it is way beyond that.

Flow state is a performance mode that personal development folks often refer to. What I am talking about is not a state that you only use for performances. I am talking about the forever flow of life itself, something more powerful than the body and mind bio hacking trend of performance junkies.

The forever flow is the earth's powers at our disposal. I have seen that I can access it when I let go of the illusions of the mind and allow life to express itself through me. That me overthinking my dance moves or what I am about to say is gone, and this playful yet powerful me takes over.

Do we say that plants are in the flow state? Do we say that the sun is shining today, so it's in flow? Do we say that our digestive organs are in a flow state when the food in our mouth comes out of our rear end?

We would say that something is wrong if that mechanism wasn't happening, wouldn't we? So I am talking about living through the natural state of potency, intuition and vibrancy that is running through everything, the thing we access when we move the obstacles out of the way.

Those obstacles of my psychological self, the one that wants to "look good" or avoid looking bad. That measurement of what the right answer is at school, wanting to get it right so it's validated as "a good boy" or girl. Our birthright and natural essence are beyond all of that, and that's what I am inviting you to come back to, by digging deep and searching inside for that powerful light cannon.

Can you feel it? Take 90 seconds right now to put the book down and sense inside yourself. Sense the energy of everything I've said so far about the expression centre and find it inside yourself.

You may find it uncomfortable, or blissful, but either way, the experience is yours so that you can measure where you are with this. I can't tell you; you live inside you–you tell me what you feel.

Learning to express my power out of C5 has been one of the most exhilarating and scary things, like the awe of a rollercoaster. It's like the feeling of vomiting but the opposite, pure ecstasy in the act of releasing my energy outwards.

As if the vomit was the essence of me beaming out of me, like sun rays. In fact, everything I've said so far is about the expression of solar rays. We have solar power inside of us, scientifically, and the sun which beams bright has an important job–to light up the world.

Chasing Fruit Vs Eating Right Now

As we shine the lifeforce through C5, we can start moving upward toward the next centre, C6. Everything is going to start making more sense at our next stop.

Before we move on, let me make this clear, I don't know if we can fully release the challenges that come up in life. Even if you think you are done, there is more. Life keeps moving, and we must keep having team meetings with our power centres so they are adapting to each new season and stage in our life.

Think of power centre development as levels with no limit, rather than completion goals. Completion goals when it comes to the personal empowerment world are created by an intellectual mind, the mind that sees things as finite.

I have allowed myself to be fooled into believing that I was "done" many times. "I am enlightened!" I thought. Then I scratched my head when I was faced with a challenge. Now I surrender into realising that life just gets better and better; I will forever be a student, and this means that I am open to various depths of development as and when they come, instead of chasing them.

Chasing some fruit in the future means we are hungry in the moment. Eating the fruit of now means we are fed right now, and we can continue farming and exploring new lands to see which fruits may bear in the future, without a desperate scarcity mentality.

I love farming fruit, I love eating fruit and I love to stumble upon fruit by surprise.

A Unified Viewing Centre

With this fed way of operating, there is a lightness as well as a discipline that will allow for an exponential development in the C5 department. With that growth, we/you (Shakti/the power) can have a stronger bond with the source and unify with it.

This is what being in alignment means, the ultimate alignment.

From here yin and yang (you, your energy) can go and dance off into the sky. That's my metaphor to lead us into the next chapter.

Life gets exciting when the parts inside us meet and come into union because there is a one-pointed view, a centredness that occurs in our way of operating. The mind becomes balanced, and useful as a tool.

Once I began to experience this way of life, I began to see that ultimate bliss is inside of us and I have looked all over the world and through all sorts of habits to find it. This discovery helped me drop tons of the pleasure-based habits I held onto, effortlessly.

When I tasted the bliss of personal alignment, command, and unification, I saw pleasure as a weak substitute. It's like eating mud when you can eat chocolate, unless you are into mud that is.

I will explain what I mean in the next chapters.

✏️ Questions to consider:

Which challenges do you face when expressing yourself confidently?

What would you like to express outwardly as an expression of the inside? Remember this doesn't have to be direct speech, it can be a new phase in your life, a business, it can be helping others, having better relationships, or whatever your inner power is longing to experience on the outside.

Do you ever feel physical discomfort in your throat or chest? Is there a mental/energetic reason for this?

What do you do to train your freedom muscle?

If you were lecturing students on the meaning of "Your Full Expression", how would you describe it to them in one paragraph?

Remember, these answers are for you, and unique to you.

I encourage you to look for the absolute truth, beyond the distorted mind illusions.

C6 - The Vision Centre - The Power of The Lighthouse

Chakra Name: *Ajna*
Sanskrit Meaning: *Commander*
Location: *Above the Mid of the Eyebrows (Third Eye)*
Elemental Power: *Light*

"In order to be who you are, you must be willing to let go of who you think you are."
~ Michael A. Singer

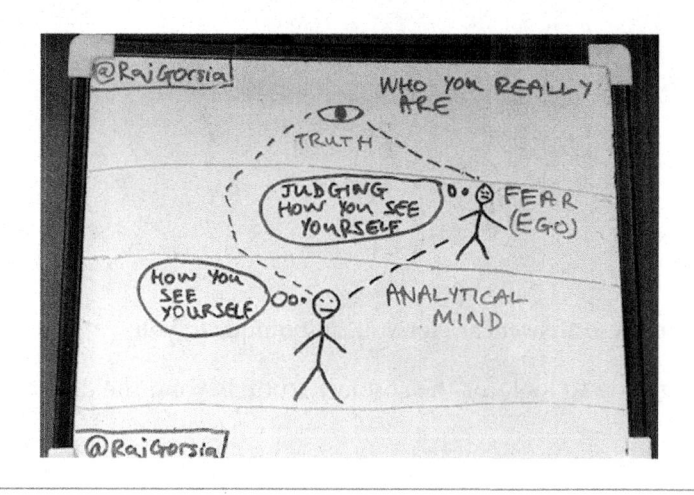

I started experiencing a tingling sensation in my third eye centre before I even knew what a chakra or power centre was, before I even started meditating or knew anything about inner energy. It came when I started practicing a weekly yoga class that was arranged by my work's well-being team.

I didn't have any intention when going to this class apart from trying out something new that may help me with my physical performance. The "gym bro" way of looking at it, I also went because I liked one of the girls who was going, the mind of a 25-year-old man. Little did I know what that yoga class would have led me towards: an earth-shattering level of awakening.

You may be wondering; how did you experience C6 if the root (C1) is at the bottom and the journey is upwards? That doesn't make sense Raj.

Well, remember that throughout this book I have said that Shakti (the active lifeforce) is moving towards Shiva (the still source), the calling is happening from C6 and above. It's like Shakti has a compass pointed in a particular direction so she knows where to go.

Shakti is magnetically and naturally drawn to Shiva because that's where the wholeness and the source is. Yin and yang signify two parts of a whole becoming one. The ultimate destiny being one, because they are one. This is what yoga, taoism, tantra and most spiritual or religious teachings are about.

I realised for myself that separation is experienced for a reason, for us to yearn for becoming one again. You can call that spiritual awakening, you can call it thrill chasing or searching for meaning in life, whatever works for you. It's a longing to become unified, dressed in different manifestations.

The vision centre signals this to us, as well as providing the mechanism for unification to occur. It's like a motherboard on a personal computer that is connected to the overall network.

* * *

Morse Code From The Source Code

This is the wisdom that my experience was pointing towards, I felt the tingling, it persisted, and my whole world began to change. The forehead tingling was directing me towards an invisible path in the direction of my inner compass. Almost like Morse code in the forehead, tapping away through thoughts, sensations, and experiences.

Of course, most of it was unconscious, I did not have anyone telling me what was happening, and I did not even have a logical understanding of it. It was more of a subtle knowing that was telling me to explore and explore, to experiment and see. Like when you know which outfit to buy, where does that choice come from?

The third eye is like a beacon, a solar flare that has been lit, a knowing where to go. Shiva does not go down to meet Shakti in the ground, he sits there in meditation and stillness, and he is inviting her back home to him. A beacon doesn't have a purpose to move, it sits still–so you have a direction, doesn't it?

Shakti (our dynamic lifeforce) came from Shiva, he is the silent unborn all and she is the active and alive manifestation of the source. Shiva represents the still conscious intelligence and nothingness that we came from, and Shakti represents the powerful moving spark of everything. Two sides to life. In breath and out breath.

Remember to put aside your mind's gender beliefs beside here. This book is only an attempt to put the illogical into words, so put all of your mental constructs about life to the side and invite in your connection to an innate intelligence.

The source of life is beyond gender and form, I am using the reference "him" and using the characters of male and female in this love story format for a reason, because we understand it easier that way, don't we?

We could not be born if there were no parts. This is not about gender; see past gender, see past any idea that you might form when I talk about "*the woman*" coming to "*the man*". Once again, this isn't about physical images, mental morals, beliefs, ethics or relationship psychology. We are looking beyond psychology and sociology.

Life-intelligence doesn't have a psychological mind. I am inviting you to look at this on a spiritual science level. The modern day scientists will be able to relate to what I am saying but they will explain it in a different way.

I say all of this because it's exactly what I had to do to access deeper wisdom beyond my intellect. My mind was trying to push everything away like a backhand in tennis, hitting it away so it could protect its current level of knowledge. "How how how" it asks.

The Lighthouse Inside

If someone is focusing their existence on the lower centres and living based on their psychological and physical structures alone then the lifeforce energy of Shakti will go around in circles and less amounts of her powers will be able to move in other directions.

However, even if someone isn't consciously activating their energy flow, Shakti can still ascend if she is really tuned into the calls and solar flares being let off by Shiva from above. It's the level of potency and awareness that varies with development, as well as how we are influenced and react to the blocks that get awakened along the way.

There's a whole chain reaction occurring within us when we access new insight and new energy. The thing I struggled with most was how to work with it and make sense of it.

It began happening for me in very tiny ways, ways that I did not really understand. I was becoming aware of the signals and the new way of seeing that were available to me, and I started saying yes to more things and no to more things. At the same time, I was very confused and did not know what was happening to me. A door had opened and it was kind of scary to look inside it.

In personal development circles the terms "consciousness" or "awareness" are popular these days, that is what seeing through the third eye is related to.

The ships of my mind were aimlessly moving in the sea for years, getting frustrated (like we do in life) and chasing glimpses of light but never really getting anywhere. But finally, my inner ships noticed something in the distance to move towards, a lighthouse that kept turning on over and over, so their radars switched on and the captain knew in his heart that it was the right way to go.

That was the pulsing sensation I began to feel in my head from those yoga classes–that was the Morse code signals.

I began having a direction for the first time in my life and it was leading me somewhere, even if I did not have a map or understanding of what I would face along the way. The lighthouse itself was enough to give me some bearings.

* * *

I used to say, "I wish I knew this ages ago!" as it would have saved me so much suffering throughout my life, but I am now wise enough to cherish the beauty of the process. It happened when it needed to happen, and it unraveled on its own in a naturally messy and perfectly imperfect way.

No amount of intellectual knowledge could have allowed me to experience this awakening differently than I did. I did not have any guidance from anyone to help me, I went about it in an unorthodox way through isolation, confusion and a lot of trial and error over a long period of time. I did not want to ask for help (ego got in the way), so I went on an experimental path and it happened how it did, eventually creating insights for me because I was committed to moving towards the lighthouse.

I am so passionate about helping people now because I know that some level of guidance from the right person would have been helpful. I had so many unanswered questions, time spent, and feelings that I didn't understand. The lighthouse seemed scary, it kept turning on and off and I hesitated in going towards it.

Having the right person there may have helped me to move through the process more efficiently, so I am here to give people what I wish I had through this book and through everything I do.

Perhaps we can say, being the co-captain on the ship.

Unified Action

C6 is highly important because it's the caller, and without it, nothing else would be possible. It's the anchor, the commander, the wise leader within the human. When I connect to it, I have oversight of my whole way of operating, and I can consciously turn up the level of potency of the other centres at will. If I am disconnected, then everything becomes a cloudy mess, and it feels like the lighthouse isn't there.

Being a computer nerd for most of my life, I love to learn how my inner operating system covers both the logical and creative sides of looking at things. It's like seeing a computer which has a 3D screensaver, I can figure out the logic of how it's made, whilst also being awestruck at its creative inception.

The creative inception of screensavers came from a guy called John Socha, he created the whole thing in his head and then figured out the logic to turn it into reality. That is the third eye at its best, it unites parts of our intelligence so that they can work together to create things into form. Mind as a powerful tool, versus a wild horse running around in circles.

My mind was definitely a wild horse for most of my life, and still takes me to that place from time to time, until I plug back into the masterful sixth centre.

C6 puts the mind into focus, and it recruits all parts of us to add to the joint effort. The body was involved when the guy made the screen saver; he had to type up the code, he had to do something that nobody has ever done before. Courage was required, and kindness to himself must have been required too.

The vision centre puts everything into correct alignment, like various strings coming together, led by one hand, the master's hand. Your hand.

A Unified Mind

We can also say that C6 represents intuition and higher knowing, and by that, I mean the ability to envision with higher clarity and understanding, beyond the psychological mind and physical body.

It goes beyond the safety responses and the identity, and it calls in all of our dimensions of intelligence at once so that they can be transformed and combined into a one-pointed sharper intelligence. That's why it's one eye– it doesn't separate, it brings it all together.

In Yogic science the mind is said to be made of four main parts: Consciousness, Intellect, Ego, and Memories. A unified mind is one that has the ability to think with poise, without being undermined by our memories, fears and the identity that we have created through our thinking.

The vision centre helps us take all parts into account and observes their views, but it is not attached to any of them. It is like a wise judge who hears all parties before making a decision.

This beautiful mode of seeing allows us to see fresh and new, it's like clear white paint untouched by any other colors. I believe that's why it's called a third eye, it sees things without being biased on left or right sides of us, like a parent who cannot choose a favorite child out of two and loves them both.

What I ended up discovering through meditative experience was that the third eye represents a personal experience of life that is beyond duality. This is a huge topic but let me simplify it by saying that we tend to see the world through our psychological mind and our creative essence. Both of them dance with the outside world, the sensations, and create experiences for us.

I was indecisive throughout my entire life and it was one of the biggest stress creators of my life because I did not know how to best deal with the experiences I was having or which of my inner perspective to listen to. I was torn apart, definitely not unified in my way of operating, and spending energy by over-analysing everything and fighting with myself.

I was traveling around South America for three months and I had bought a return flight from Brazil to London. I rushed through the continent to ensure that I "stuck to the plan" and could catch my flight back home. But when I arrived in Brazil I felt a feeling of unease. I did not want to go home, it felt like I was not done.

The intellectual mind was saying "You've got a ticket home already paid for, just go and you can travel again another time in life". The present moment intelligence was saying "Who cares about the ticket, forget about it". I ended up staying.

This is just one example of when I have been torn inside, but it's also happened throughout my life. Within my career, with the next steps in life, with actions I wanted to take, with relationships, with business, and anything else you can think of. Even simple things like choosing whether to go out or not.

There's often a war going on inside and it can create so much inner turmoil and judgment. Often the intellectual mode wins because we choose "what makes sense" and is safe, but the third eye represents a way of seeing that allows us to see with clarity and listen to both sides.

It is not always smart to quit our jobs and start a business, sometimes it's smarter to have a side hustle until the business pays off (like I did). C6 allows us to see in a truly intelligent way, beyond emotional reactions.

Unifying in C6 allows for the mechanism of working as a unified force in everyday life. Shiva and Shakti, mind, and body, right and left side of our bodies, universal and personal, inside and outside, intuition and action, still and dynamic.

* * *

I now see why I felt tingling as my first experience of the centres switching on. It's because this caller–this lighthouse–was trying to tell me to align the bricks in my life. Have you ever seen a Jenga board? When you first lay it out, it's so straight that it doesn't fall, but after playing around with it over time it starts to get misaligned and shaky.

That's us, we can spend a lifetime making moves on our Jenga board of life and pulling things out of alignment, and then leaving them like that because we've gotten used to it as being our "normal". Like a misaligned spine.

Thankfully for us, we don't need to stay like that or wait until we fall. We can make reverse Jenga moves, putting things into alignment. That's what I've enjoyed doing with my life, in every area, with every part of myself, with C6 being the intelligence that drives that activity.

And guess what, I am not done. I am working on it over and over, I may accidentally knock the pieces over a few times, but I know how they fit together. Like teaching my nephew how to reassemble the Jenga when we start again, he knows how it goes, so he knows how to reset and realign it.

The game of life is to be played from this eye, and for me it's the most freeing way to live.

* * *

Move Sharp

Notice how you have two eyes, two sides of the brain, two arms, and two legs. Through the power centres we have one pointed energy headquarters which reside in the centre of specific areas along our spine.

They are in the centre of left and right because they are all individually and collectively working towards the ultimate goal of unity.

Even logically and in the sense of geometrical design, it's satisfyingly sensible. Like seeing the architecture of a building. One building, different parts, working together for one purpose.

As a wing chun master once said to me, "strike powerfully when you want to but whilst being relaxed, not tense". He went on to explain to me how smooth wing chun (life) can be when we know how to relax instantly and how to be explosive instantly, dancing between the two. He blew my mind.

Like a sword that has a sharp blade and a smart swordsman. The sword has no purpose without the wielder, and the swordsman is not a swordsman if he doesn't use the sword. It's like being a motorbike fanatic, wearing a leather jacket and looking the part but never actually riding a motorbike.

The mind and the body, the tact and the action must become one and dance in unity for us to live at our potential.

If we can harness all our inner instruments and use them in the world with a graceful intensity, we are living our purpose as humans.

The wisdom we can access through the vision centre can help us see that. It's the eyes beyond the eyes, it's the detached action and the detached thinking.

Beyond The Intellectual

Shiva represents "that which is not", the nothingness, the unmanifested. It's something that we don't know but we do, which means our intellect doesn't recognize it, but a higher wisdom inside us does.

If we try to intellectualise this force, then we will miss the point completely. It's like trying to describe the taste of an apple, can you do it and really give someone an experience of it through your definition?

As the Tao te Ching says "The Tao that can be told is not the eternal Tao. The name that can be named is not the eternal name". Zen uses koans, sufis use poems, and other traditions use their own ways to get us into felt experience versus intellectual thinking.

From my experience, I have found it to be way more intelligent to use deduction as a way of connecting to this space of nothingness. If I say, "I am not the body, I am not the mind, I am not the energy, I am not the heart, I am nothing that I think I am", it helps me to create insight into what I am not and see that what's left is what I am, without describing it.

If I attached to a description "Ah ha, I'm sure, this is what it is!" then I would be using the intellect, the very thing that limits me from seeing beyond it to experience what I am. It's a little confusing perhaps, and very nuanced, but does that make sense?

The same logic applies to understanding the power of the third eye. I have had many moments when I "just knew" that something was a good choice even if logic gave me 1000 reasons not to go there. It was a felt sense.

It's Inner Sight versus Intellect, it's Knowing versus Knowledge.

Can you think of some examples for yourself?

* * *

No Rush

The knowing trumps the knowledge, when has information alone really helped someone to smile, or to act courageously, or to be at peace, or to love?

The vision centre creates the possibility to see things from a wiser and higher vantage point. This higher view gives us the power to stand over the chessboard and see which moves we want to make without fear stopping us.

If you've seen any of my talks or YouTube videos, you'll notice that I speak without rush, and I take pauses between my words. That's because I am allowing the intelligence to speak. It's calm, centred, intuitive, and I am not thinking about what to say.

Stepping into this mode has allowed me to make the most effective gear shifts in my life. I go into the driver's seat and have all the buttons and controls in front of me without being worried about how to drive.

As my dad used to say to me "Why are you rushing?!" I used to think "This old man's got too much time on his hands". But he was right, there's no need to rush when I am composed. When I have a firm grasp on life through this centred view, it allows me to see the biggest insight of my life, which is asking the question "What do I think is running out?" It's moved me from living in scarcity to living from a place of fulfillment being in every moment.

I can still drive fast, faster perhaps, but I am focused and present because I am not thinking too much, I am in focus and flow, like a top race car driver must be. Without focus, they are just reckless drivers with a higher risk of crashing. This analogy works the same for everyday life, personally and professionally.

Potential Blocks

Waldo vs Odlaw

When I had a cover over my third eye and energy flow, I could not see anything beyond my intellectual knowledge or emotional reactions. I only saw what I could prove or analyse through the psychological eye.

There was a girl who was helping me overcome my inner block, you can call her a mentor but I'd say she was an angel. She kept trying to help me, but all I did was ask her logical questions like "How does this work? What's the science behind it?".

And hey these questions are OK, but I realised that they were a cover-up for my fear of being vulnerable and letting go of my hungry need for control. Not letting things in.

A philosopher trying to figure out life through their intellect will never understand life because the intellect (as hard as it tries) doesn't control the present moment. It's off-duty then because it only works on moving toward something, not staying still.

I used to wonder why I could not move past my inner challenges by thinking about it, in fact I used to wonder why it was so hard and stressful. Why wasn't it easy?

It's because the fear response was triggered so the tool of the intellect was receiving that data and was switching on all the alarms in the body. It's like a danger signal being switched on to alert that the driver is panicking (or has fallen asleep) so the autopilot has to take over and drive.

This autopilot computer is built for protection from death, so it will enhance its systems for the purpose of preserving the car.

What I learnt though, is that this system can operate in situations that are less subtle than a full-blown panic situation, and sometimes it's on when I think I am right, sometimes it's on when I am active or talking to someone. This is the ego form of fear, it's so alluring and concealed.

It takes a sharp eye to catch it out, like finding Wally/Waldo. Once you see it, your whole energy changes, and there's freedom from working so hard.

It's no wonder that desperately and constantly asking questions to ourselves can feel draining. We are looking for Waldo all day long.

The frantic mind doesn't know where to find him, so it keeps circling around and eventually thinks there is a problem because it doesn't know where he is. It then blames us or others and gets angry at the game (of life).

Or the intellect convinces us that we found him (found an answer or conclusion about life) so we live through an illusion of it. It isn't really Waldo though, it's often his nemesis, Odlaw. Oh yeah, the psychological mind can be very smart, it can align us with the devil and make us believe it's the angel.

That's why awareness through the vision centre is key; it allows our discernment and purest of wisdom to see the truth and destroy illusion. Shiva is often called the destroyer in Hinduism.

The most useful way for me to look at this role of his is to see him as the destroyer of illusion, of drama, of ego. To bring me/us into ease, truth and clarity.

Tune Into That Station

Imagine trying to ask a robot to give you answers, all it knows is the programming that it has received. We gathered our intellectual algorithms through life experiences, often during childhood.

So the intellect is blind in the sense that it isn't intelligent like our true intelligence which is infinitely creating new possibilities.

It's like falling over as a kid, the kid just gets up and brushes it off. They have such powerful resilience and bounce back, it doesn't matter what anyone else says, the kid is sure of themselves.

Like my nephew who hands me his drawings and says it's a house. It looks like scribbles to me, but he is sure it's a house–that's his creative confidence shining.

The natural intelligence that we were born out of, which sustains life on this planet works in every moment, and it's the most powerful force in the world. Is anything more powerful? So it must be the same for us, for us to access the most powerful force in the world we must be completely aware of the in-moment intelligence. Tune into it, over and over.

It's like tuning into a radio with those old school knobs that you have to turn. To get to 95.8 FM, I must move the tuner until it's just right, a little left, and a little right, until I've found the sweet spot.

That is what we are able to do too, find that centre point of clarity and hear the sounds of intelligence moving through us. That's what C6 does, it tunes the entire system into alignment.

* * *

Knowledge Versus Knowing

This thinking tool is amazing because it helps us create magic in the world, but it becomes a problem when our fear projections block the magical creativity of our lives.

I was stuck in my psychology for a lot of my life, constantly researching, looking at science, analyzing, and trying to find the "right answer", rather than listening to any wisdom of my own. I was trying to measure up to the opinions and operating models, so there wasn't an opportunity to live through my own authenticity or establish trust in myself.

Looking at how others do things and attempting to copy them is like wearing someone else's clothes–it's a little weird, isn't it? It's like when you copy someone's homework at school, you can get an A grade for the exam, but you will not feel the satisfaction of working your personal intelligence muscle. It feels good to find solutions, doesn't it? Like creating a pump in the gym.

All I was doing when I was collecting knowledge was feeding a hunger for the "right answer" on paper, to feel like I've accomplished an understanding of the topic. It's like dancing, no matter how many dance books I read, I will never understand dance through theoretical knowledge.

So knowledge isn't power to me, but experimenting with the knowledge to gain experienced knowing? That is power. There is a subtle distinction.

It's super important to learn from the outside sources, otherwise an egoic isolation can occur, but for me the key is fusing everything from the outside with my inner intelligence, staying true to my dance moves rather than trying to dance like someone else.

As a quick exercise, make an audit of the things that you intellectually learn or know a lot about that you would like to experience as a true living reality.

I know I had a lot, for example, peace, career success, confident speaking, better relationships, amazing health, courage, action without hesitation, and tons more.

People often quote famous people, "the power of now" or Indian sages, and tell me that they want to experience what they speak of, not just logically take it in. Well, there's a pathway. It's all about willingness, and the "big buts" that get in your way.

Defensive Mind And The Big Butt

Other blocks that I faced were along the lines of not trusting my intuition or trusting anothers support, which again could connect with the root centre and lack of safety, or perhaps a closed connection centre.

I've felt this one a lot and it sometimes still comes up if I am not in a place of poise within myself. I have gotten angry at people because I felt that they were judging or undermining me. I would rather have suffered than take the higher perspective and let someone in.

I now know that even if it sounded like they were judging me, the ownership is on me to bring myself down and equally up, not anyone else. That gives me great freedom, to know that my reactions are mine.

It's when I am tuned into my C6 awareness that I am able to best see that, otherwise I will walk around like a victim to my own mind and to other people.

The left and right side become split, rather than together as a centralised team.

It's really easy to get into a stubborn trance and to block everyone out, like putting physical barriers up so nobody can get near. Hey I've done it, that's why I write all of these words, I've faced it all.

Even if someone is being kind, if we aren't centred and seeing intelligently, the body and mind will take the driver's seat. It's like being possessed, perhaps being possessed is someone moving off their centre and getting caught up in the mind and body reactions, rather than an actual external force possessing them.

Getting caught in the mind and body programs doesn't need judgment though, we all do it.

I realized that we protect our mind limitations, we feed the monkey bananas as I say. Even if we get to a place of centred vision, we end the sentence with a but. We say but, but, but, and we get in our own way. It's like cutting out the lights out to our own party.

When I am coaching someone and I see them cutting out their own light, I might cheekily ask. "Is your but in the way?"

It's like a person with a big behind, knocking things over as they move around.

Like a bull in a china shop, the but is so big sometimes that all of the china is falling and we are looking around to see why it's happening, often unaware of our blind spot, the big but that's knocking it over.

It's funny isn't it? We can add humour to this so that it's more of a freedom creator than a shaming exercise. My clients often relax when we catch their big but, and they see beyond it and laugh towards a calmer way of operating because the alarm system gets shut down.

I love to bring humor to my life and to my teachings, it brings me back home and simplifies the lesson because it unlocks the security gate, and escorts me into the elevator of my headquarters, letting me see things from the highest level.

Would You Eat Pavement?

I realise now why it took this tingling in my head to spark the journey I went on. It's because I was beginning to see the world 1% differently for the first time, and it allowed me to see new choices despite the fears I had.

It allowed me to let go of analysing how good/bad an experience would be and instead just being with the experience. It allowed me to go beyond the head's convincing knowns and try out the unknowable.

After living a life that felt dark at times, it felt amazing to see life 5% brighter. That 5% can make a difference can't it? It's like a phone screen, there's more clarity when it's brighter.

I see that when people are stuck in their ways, acting stubborn and closed, it kills the buzz of life inside them, their whole aura goes low, like having a blender with a low-power motor. The insides are lumpy, not smooth. We need to check that there isn't a hard piece in there clogging the motor, perhaps going to the core centre and boosting its power, or checking the others centres.

It's hard to see clearly when there is a clog in the energy flow, smoke starts to generate and gets in our eyes. Sometimes we aren't even aware of it, it just seems like it's "me", or it's "normal".

I found a lot of unconscious sheets in the basement of my mind that were covering up the real me and telling him what an "acceptable way to be" was.

My acceptable way was to be a nice boy who doesn't step outside of the "rules", because it's shameful to do so. My acceptable way was really to avoid being confident because I saw it as a repulsive trait.

We are much more intelligent than our psychological ideas of our "self". Wisdom isn't a trait that is based on a collection of knowledge, that's fake wisdom, that's the ego's playground.

True wisdom is tapping into sensing and knowing. It's being tuned into oneself, others, and everything else around us. Seeing with a unified eye.

* * *

Why do fear-driven emotions and thinking hurt so much? Why does it create this term called "stress"? Stress for me was when my mind was taking me out of harmony inside, causing my body to get confused and heat up or cool down to try and resolve the confusion. The buttons were being pressed inside, flickering between fight, flight, freeze or frustration.

The room temperature is what we want to naturally come back to. That is the state of being that is naturally balanced, unified, and calm. When the mind controls us, we go into a different temperature based on the ideas in our heads rather than raising the temperature for a reason.

For example, if our nervous system was fired up for an actual fight to occur, then great, go ahead and switch everything on. But when it happens in situations where there is no actual threat, the mind gets confused and tries to scan and support the situation, but there's nothing for it to do, so it goes around in circles. The energy is not mobilised.

That's why it hurts, because it isn't natural. It's like putting too much air into a balloon, the pressure builds once it's too much, and it isn't natural. It's natural to let go of some air and glide through like that perfectly blown balloon.

No wonder it feels so good to hear Goldilocks' story, we know what the middle bed of "just right" feels like as a way of operating in life.

I sometimes use the example of eating an apple when I speak about natural versus unnatural way of operating. An apple naturally feels good to eat and our bodies feel good when it's inside of us. We just know it, by tasting it, by looking at it, by even feeling its texture.

If you went and ate the pavement, it wouldn't feel good or feel natural. In the same way, we just know. Even walking on pavement or walking on grass, we can feel the difference between what is natural and what is not. People have even started practices like "barefoot grounding" to get in touch with the natural energy that I am talking about.

* * *

This same logic works for the way we lead our life. If we use the third eye then we can see our highest way of operating because it plugs us into an intelligence that feels "just right".

It's like checking to see if your soup is warm enough to drink, you know by feeling into it, rather than mentally calculating.

Practicing this way of operating was the only way that I could move past the challenges in my head and the torment that I faced. I sat in my room resentful and ruminating over little situations that occurred in my everyday life. All whilst sitting still in my room.

Imagine looking at it as a reality TV show, it would look strange. Why is this person so tense when nothing is happening? It's easy to hide that stuff from the outside because it was all happening inside the maze of my body-mind TV show.

I was so attached to analysing and scaring myself because of it. When I learned to raise my awareness beyond the body and mind, I found ways to access a breath that felt like receiving CPR, to become alive again.

C6 allows us to see things from a unified perspective. When there is no war inside between the parts of myself and the world, then there is harmony, and the cogs all move together as a team. That is what this master power centre does, it's the inner genius.

It Isn't All Fun And Games.

Once the vision centre begins to open it can create a feeling of discomfort, because a conflict where you feel like you knew one way of the world but now you are seeing another way can ensue. It's scary because we build an identity around who we think we are, and even if we want freedom from it, it can feel challenging to let it go and let in a new way of seeing.

I know I felt tension because I began to question what was true and what wasn't. It was this scary kind of freedom. Like free diving in the ocean, there's just blue sea under you and nothing to hold onto. I am not a great swimmer so for me this example relates to feeling vulnerable and unsafe. The mind doesn't want us to let go of its strongly formed beliefs because it has upheld them for ages.

When the third eye is used it allows for us to see a dualistic way of life, but also holds the potential to go beyond it. To see beyond two, and to see one, that's why it's a third eye.

Awareness can sometimes feel scary, sometimes I wish I didn't know this stuff and didn't wake my vision centre up because I have become more sensitive to truths that sometimes feel uncomfortable. It's like when I first learned that a lot of clothes are made in sweatshops in harsh conditions, the clothes I wore looked different.

When I began to awaken into a new way of seeing, I was questioning who I was, I was feeling lost, and I was feeling resentment. It all happens as the C6's viewing centre opens. You like seeing animals, go view them at a zoo, that's one view, but another perception might open up and you get a strange feeling upon seeing the cage.

This is what inner sight is, it is viewing things differently not based on the outer senses but on an inner sense. It's the not-so-sexy part of spirituality, it is not always easy because it can feel life-altering.

I've had people tell me that they are scared to go deeper into their personal journey because they fear what they might do when they see things. They are longing for opening a door but their eyes are only a quarter open, and they are scared to touch the door handle.

It's like being scared of ghosts, or "dark energies", I think it's all influenced by the conclusions of the mind, by us. Even if I am wrong, isn't it more empowering and freeing to see it that way?

I get it though, the fear part, I've felt this too. I've scared myself off from looking, sometimes I've had a guide who's already been through to hold my hand, and sometimes I've ventured alone. Either way, it's been worth it in the end.

People can be sent into the belief that they are going crazy because of the new thoughts and inner visions they are seeing, and they have convinced themselves that they have lost the plot. But this is only happening because of the addition of a psychological layer to the consciousness expansion that is happening within them.

The truth is that all of this fresh new thinking and seeing is a viewing platform which is beyond the psychological layer, but that psyche will still get involved and try to understand what is happening by adding more layers of thinking. It's all part of the process, it was for me anyway.

I googled the symptoms of third eye-opening. Here's what came up:

"Symptoms can include: Confusion, uncertainty, cynicism, lack of purpose, pessimism."

Check, check and check, I felt all of those. Trust me though, it's worth it, we can move forward from these moments. I am not trying to scare you away. Instead I am here to inform you by sharing some of the experiences that might occur.

Beyond all that noise and once Shiva and Shakti meet, there will be an illuminating feeling going through the body. I remember feeling these jerking electrical pleasure shocks running all the way up my spine. These were my first reactions when my body was trying to help me to unify.

I now know that it was happening because things were trying to unblock, like during a massage when a knot is released and a gentle "ahhhh" proceeds. It doesn't always feel that enjoyable to release those knots though does it, but it's all for a great purpose.

I didn't really understand it at the time, but these sensations were a result of energy connecting with awareness, for a micro-moment. It was the known meeting the unknown, the movement meeting the stillness, the masculine and the feminine; it felt like a celebration, fireworks at a party. It is a party because the forces of Shiva and Shakti, your energy and your awareness are joining together in all their glory.

Experiencing high levels of aliveness mixed with high levels of awareness is a feeling of complete empowerment. No wonder drug makers made things to try and replicate it. Fully present and still, whilst totally charged, that's a cocktail at a bar that I like to be at.

It's unmatched. In yogic science, this can perhaps be described as the jump-off for experiencing Samadhi, which can be experienced once we go beyond the self-limitations and unify with a supreme energy.

A Sanskrit term I love to live by and embody is "sat-chit-ananda", which means being true conscious bliss. Shakti as the bliss creating energy, Shiva as the true intelligence, and you conscious of being that blissful truth in your life, it's a delightful way of operating.

Sat-chit-ananda. You are that.

It's our birthright to use this way of being as a superpower, one that destroys all limitations and creates all possibilities.

When I started entering into this realm of operating, I was boomed into the sky, whilst being present for the whole ride.

Athletes, leaders, artists, performers, and race car drivers are looking for a version of this, they know that if they can be fully conscious and use their energy from a place of precision, anything is possible.

Summary Of C6

C6 is the master because it's the one that can see all the other centres. It's the watcher, the one that knows all and sees all. It plugs in and takes intelligence directly from the source, the unknowable, the divine.

It's the bridge between personal and universal. If this centre is really focused then you can experience what the sages, masters, and yogis experience: life-flowing intelligence.

A heightened state of intelligence comes from a heightened state of awareness. Awareness is what Buddhism and Zen talk a lot about.

Buddhism is taken from Hinduism, and it's popular because it's very practical and easy to understand and implement. I aim to make my sharings simple too; sharing my own experience whilst adding logic, modern structure, story, and relevancy so it's more easily accessible than ancient teachings may be.

Stoicism and a lot of modern philosophy are reason and thought-focused. It feeds the intellect of people and makes them feel like they have an understanding of their life. Men especially seem to love this path.

I too have found it really useful but I want to go deeper into the chemistry to have a holistic understanding, that's what yogic sciences provide me. For me, uniting body, heart, mind, elements, and everything else is way more useful than reasoning alone.

The yogic system (in my opinion and experience) takes everything to another level, and accounts for every way of looking at things whilst being extremely scientific.

It provides amplification of both consciousness and lifeforce power and joins them into one force. It considers the elements, astrological cycles, geometry, gastronomy, and all sorts of other scientific systems.

Isn't that cool? And despite there being so many different branches, everything is connected to a oneness, it's beautiful.

This is what the vision centre has the potential to show us–how to connect the dots, whilst bringing them all into one. C6 has the vision to let us see the algorithm of life. Like the matrix.

* * *

So now we have talked about being guided by the inner lighthouse, what's next? Well, the party really begins now. It's the final centre that holds the superpower to let go of everything and experience the light show.

But not only as the watcher, not only as the power of lifeforce (Shakti), not only through personal unification but as an entity beyond that. We get to surrender ourselves. Back to where we came from.

I look forward to being your tour guide to take you there.

To no-where.

Where there's no map.

✏ Questions to consider:

When you are feeling your calmest and sharpest, what have you been able to see that you might not have seen before? Think of a few examples.

What happens when you bring your awareness to your third eye area and take 10 breaths into it? Don't think it. Test it, like trying foods.

What do you think the vision centre is useful for, in your own words?

What did you take away from this chapter, and what do you wish to explore further?

C7 - The Crown Centre - The Power of Letting Go

Chakra Name: *Sahasara*
Sanskrit meaning: *Infinity*
Location: *Top of the Head (Crown)*

"Letting go is like the sudden cessation of an inner pressure or the dropping of a weight. It is accompanied by a sudden feeling of relief and lightness, with an increased happiness and freedom. It is an actual mechanism of the mind, and everyone has experienced it on occasion."
~ David R. Hawkins

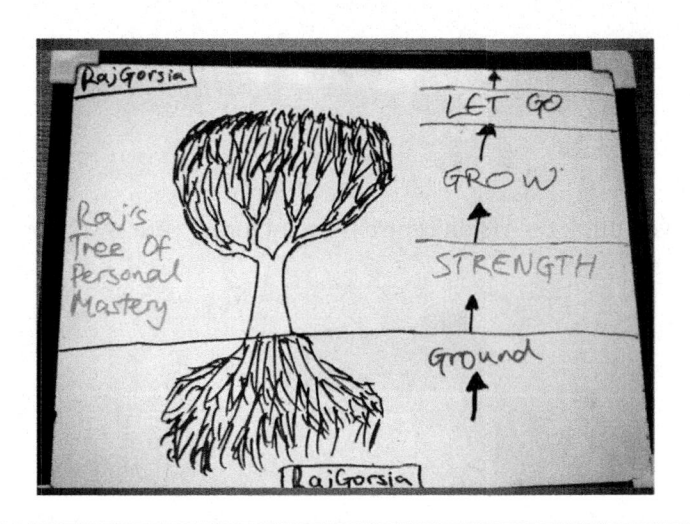

The crown centre is different to the other centres. It sits on top of our brain like a crown that we can wear (the clue is in the name).

If you google the chakras it will tell you the same. For me, it was not logic-based knowledge that told me that though, it was more of an experienced knowing during my development process. Again, I say this not to show off but to lead you towards the path of experiential learning rather than theory-based knowledge storing.

Try this out right now. Close your eyes for 60 seconds and see if you can sense an antenna-like feeling above your head, one that tunes you into the world outside of you. You might not feel it, or you might, don't know until you try right?

* * *

What Does Wearing This Crown Give Me?

I was sitting in meditation one lush summer's day under a tree (Buddha style) and I had a sharp sensation through the top of my head. The insight hit me that the crown centre's purpose is to provide me with a connection to a power beyond my "self". It's not about us as a self, an individual. It's not about our physical experience, and it's not even about our connection with our life experience. It's different to the heart centre in that sense.

The crown centre is the connection to something greater than the eyes can see and the brain can fathom. It's the doorway to ultimate freedom.

Take the example of being at a concert. My experience is what I see and feel, but the crown centre plugs me into what the entire concert feels. The people, the sounds, the colours, the weather, the space in which the concert is occupying, and the entire atmospheric existence. It represents the everything, the fabric of it all, all at once.

It might not sound like a superpower, but I know that if I am plugged into this supreme plug, then I can let go of my desire to hold onto things, I can let go of a desire of even love, of even feeling alive, of my body, of my mind, of everything.

How It Feels

It feels like falling into a never-ending pit of nothingness, one where the feeling of a fall is just an illusion that represents letting go of the mind once and for all. Only the mind thinks it's falling, because its purpose is to preserve us as a separate self. Only the senses see images and experience this physical world, beyond them there is something else.

The Power Centres

When we plug into C7 we let go of needing to see things from a personal perspective, instead we see it from a place which knows nothing, is nothing, but is everything and knows everything all at once.

When I began to experience this, I was stunned into silence. A silence like no other, not even personal silence or human silence anymore. But a silence like I was dying and all I could see and feel was the bliss of light. But not light, and not dark either, not even Raj Gorsia anymore. Something without words.

I guess this is why near-death experience stories are described as going to "heaven", "towards the light", and "so freeing". If we access something beyond the container of mind and body, imagine how liberating that must feel?

How can death be scary if we go beyond body and mind? All our perceptions of problems exist in the world of mind and body. Beyond that, we are free.

This is what I felt, the feeling of death, and aliveness, at once. It was stunning. I understood why all the near-death experiences reported it being a bliss like no other, because I was experiencing it for myself through meditation and then coming back to my body and mind with a freshness like no other. Like a reset of a computer, a rebirth.

From these experiences, I began to understand that the crown centre provides a gateway to surrendering into god/universe/the ultimate source, freedom, or whatever else you can use to describe what I said above.

If the vision centre was the realisation and harnessing of one's lifeforce potential through all of the other centres, then the crown centre is entering into a space beyond the self where we dissolve back into the source of where we came from, like a brain cell that is a part of a whole body.

This is why this centre sits on top of the body, makes sense doesn't it? It's because we need some form of antenna that is beyond us. It's like holding a hand-held translation device on our heads. We translate the voice of the source into ourselves.

Beyond Boundaries

Imagine a boundary between your body and another's, your body and the outside, your mind and another person's mind. When you are wearing the hat of the crown centre you see everything as nothing and everything as something at the same time. It all blends into one.

Like using a prism to see that all the colors of rainbow come from one light that's split up. This may be why the crown centre can be related to a "brilliant white light", whereas the other centres have colors.

It's like the vision centre's perception of oneness, but a level above it where the observer even disappears and there is nothing left. Everything's gone. Total release.

Our minds will do whatever it takes to resist this state because it's so used to controlling a separate self. I have had numerous experiences where my mind has made up stories of bad vibes in the room and dark energies. At first it caught me, and I stopped doing what I was doing because I was scared.

Eventually, I let the body shake in fear, and it passed, which sent me into a state of pure liberation. That's what I mean by transcending the body and mind, not falling victim to their innocent and natural resistances.

* * *

Plug In And Unplug As You Wish

When I want to be powerful in action and creation then I can move from my body and use my mind to support me. I can use the core centre and the others to support my earthly endeavors. I can use the vision centre to see things, and the throat to express them, with my heart bursting with passion.

And when I want to let go of everything, all of the power outlets, I can unplug them. It's like being a dancer; the dancer isn't always in motion, there are times for rest. Every muscle needs stillness and recovery after a contraction. I have to know when and how to do that with every area of my life.

This centre's release function is the superpower, like releasing a piece of clothing that is too tight from your body–it's simple, throw it off. Or pressing the ejector seat button in a car when it's about to crash. Screw the car, your wellbeing is more important, right?

Surrendering is similar to floating into death but a blissful version, our survival system doesn't understand that though, so it wants us to stay away.

My body began to drop tremendous amounts of weight, and I stopped caring about living my life, taking action or being around people. It got a little extreme if I am honest. I was transcending my lower centres but I wasn't balanced.

Despite being blissful and as light as a feather (literally and metaphorically), I wasn't fully embodied so earthly activities became hard. A lot of people having an "existential crisis" or a "spiritual awakening" might be able to relate.

During these moments, embodiment can be really useful, especially for the many who wish to have an everyday life and engage with life. Stabilising and strengthening the lower centres becomes vital.

That's how my journey has gone, it ended up happening that way naturally. Natural is the key, like natural peanut butter vs. man-made. If we try to put our minds, mind-made development on these centres, then we turn it into time spent on an illusion. Like digging for pearls in the desert, it's only ridiculous once we realise it is.

Yes, I mention working on the centres separately, but don't take that too intellectually. Look at it like artistic development, always keep in mind that the system is one piece.

Balance and coherence between all centres is the key, just as muscles would look best when there's a balanced level of muscular development across the body. If I take a step, my whole body is involved in one way or another, so I must involve the whole system.

Remember, these power centres are tools, each have their purpose and uses in life. It's easy to get off balance and misunderstand what is going on inside you, that's why I recommend speaking to someone who has significant experience backed up with theory.

The crown centre gives us access to the compass that the earth's axis spins on and the sun's intelligence beams from. What the hell else keeps everything intact so intelligently? We don't tell ourselves to breathe, what does that? Our personal mind cannot do that, only a universal intelligence does.

What I've got by strengthening my connection to the crown centre is a sigh of relief, a releasing and knowing that I can let go of control. Knowing that I don't need to mentally control or fearmonger myself. Isn't that delightful and useful? That's why I say these centres are tools, not beliefs.

And to test your tool, go and sit in silence for 10 minutes right now. Don't "try" to meditate, forget meditation.

As they say in zen, "just sit". Let go of performing, don't listen to music, don't try to escape, and definitely don't try to feel enlightened, let go of trying to change anything that you think or feel, just sit, and let your "self" go.

Enjoy the challenge. It isn't as easy as it sounds. And it isn't as hard as it sounds either, all the conclusions are just ego noise. Test vs. think.

Come back to the book once you are done.

Why Goldilocks Is the Way

Wearing the crown is letting go of the personal mind and letting in something that contains the source of everything. The body will feel an intense amount of bliss when our awareness is pointed in this way and when we are still enough to notice.

Imagine being a wave and then crashing back into the ocean and becoming the ocean again. Accessing the all, whilst being super aware and not unconscious like we are when we sleep.

I suspect that this is what happens when we sleep; we go back into the ocean, that's why it's so restorative, that ocean is like being a phone that gets plugged into the electrical socket, rather than running off battery alone.

I've only been able to experience this bliss when I allow myself to fully let go. I know it is not easy because the mind and body are chattering and busy and signaling me to do things, and I want to do things too right?

This book is not about oneness in the form of passivity and an escape from having to take action. I want us to be able to utilise all parts of life. Being separate whilst also being one, at the same time.

It's cool to want to achieve, to work on our bodies, and to be this separate self, that is why I believe we were put on this earth–to learn what we can while being in this world. So I am not here to say let go of everything and lie around meditating all day chasing enlightenment and renouncing from living.

Like Goldilocks and the three bears, sitting on the bed of only inward life has a half-life. I learned that through experience, it can create another kind of "spiritual illusion" and even escapism if not properly led.

Einstein Time

Sometimes I go into a zone and I will say to myself or a client, "It's Einstein time". To me, that is a conscious declaration to enter into a powerfully calm and genius mode of being.

I see Albert Einstein as a wise yogi more than a logical scientist. He knew that he could access a higher level of intelligence when he was able to slow his mind and body down and focus his awareness.

He also said that time is relative. I can agree and I bet you can if you find examples. By relative he means that time is dependent on how we relate to it. I.e. how conscious and calm we are in the moment. I know that when I am calm, time can pass and it can also go fast. When I am in a state of panic, it can feel like this moment of distress is forever but at the same time days can pass by quickly. Time is a beautiful construct that we live in.

I believe how much we have is less important than the quality of the time spent. One year of hell can also be one year of bliss. Two hours of quality time spent with someone is different from two hours of being distracted when with someone.

Einstein also said, "Logic will take you from A to B, imagination will take you everywhere."

He knew that logic is a limited step-by-step process, a known and calculated method, whereas imagination (which I see as intuitive intelligence) can create instant genius that is unexpected, sharp, and more effective than my psychologically constructed ideas.

My friend Einstein also said, "The intuitive mind is a sacred gift and the rational mind is a faithful servant. We have created a society that honors the servant and has forgotten the gift."

This to me points me back towards the path of surrender as opposed to being desperate to know everything through rational neediness. I know that for me, all my problems in life stemmed from this desperate need for control, so I followed tactics to uphold a false sense of power. I was living based on my rational conclusions and my body sensations. I didn't even know that there was such a thing called intuitive intelligence.

That rational mind bullied me and killjoyed a lot of opportunities because of the beliefs it held about life, egoically convinced and fearfully avoidant, all based on memory patterns.

Discovering the powers of surrender and letting go (the power of C7) has improved my levels of success, happiness, and peace because it's opened a door to a fresh way of looking at life. Beginner's mind as they say in zen.

Surrender Experiment

So let's go a little deeper. We let go and surrender every night when we lay on our beds to sleep each night. Sure, we may feel troubled and think about things during the night but eventually we let go enough to fall asleep. This is us practicing the act of surrender every day. We know how to do this.

We could die in our sleep for all we know, but we are able to let go and allow ourselves rest. We have gotten good at letting go, so anyone who tells me they cannot, I ask them if they sleep, just to remind them that they do have an ability to let go.

In yoga the final pose is always Savasana. This isn't a pose for relaxation, that's a byproduct of it. It's translated into "corpse pose", I figure they did that so that we would get it through our heads that it's time to practice dying, and then practice being reborn when we get up.

It's a time to declare that we are not our body and mind, as a practice, so that we are able to fully let go and surrender into the ground. Just the same as when we die, the body becomes ground.

Our bodies are made from the earth, so Savasana or any letting go practice is a simulation of letting go of our bodies go as we would during a peaceful death. That's why it's so relaxing, and it's why taking a deep out-breath is so relaxing, because death itself must be relaxing, don't you think?

This bliss is such a high state of living, it is why in yoga there is a layer called the bliss body – anandamaya kosha. It's a layer which goes beyond the physique, mind, and energy, it's a light that beams off our aura. People tell me all the time, "you've got an aura, your voice is so soothing", it's because I am operating from a different layer, one that is blissfully unified.

That is what surrender allows for, that is the power of the crown centre and the super power that you can use in your life. This is what people might call "out of body" experience, mixed with what I might call an "out of my mind" experience. It's freeing, and it's enjoyable.

That is why a wise yoga teacher would be appalled if a student tries to skip savasana, it's blasphemy because they are not completing the process and they are doing themselves a massive disservice and standing in the way of the possibility of freedom.

They are missing the best lesson of the class, and of life. They are saying no to letting go of control and effort because the rushed mind and its scarcity starts kicking in, and the person gives in to its tempting calls to block the act of letting go.

Savasana, like every other asana has a deeper meaning behind it, beyond the physical body. Every single posture has a deep life lesson and multi-purpose intelligence behind it. It changed the game for me to understand and practice using yoga as a holistic life tool rather than gymnastics or a performance led by my ego.

The Source Code Is Within

So how do we really define that thing which is the parent/god/source if we are the one inside it? Imagine the cell trying to understand how it's the body. It's a tricky one to wrap logic around, because it's bigger and smarter than us. No wonder scientists find this so difficult to put into equations.

The only way I have been able to understand this greater universe is to realise that the source code must live within me, so I must be a part of it. And if I am a part of it, then so must everyone else be a part of it, therefore we all have this source code.

When I go into this level of thinking, I go beyond the me me me me me, and my personal intellect, this is the only way I can access the source code. Do you get what I mean? That's what the crown centre helps us do: to form a connection to the source code, without defining it.

Why does Islam say not to think of Allah as an image? Perhaps it's because they are pointing us in the direction of god being beyond the human form and something that cannot be defined.

The Taoists said the same, they said, "The Tao that can be told is not the eternal Tao; the name that can be named is not the eternal name."

Why do Hindus have so many gods? Because they are referring to various forms of the one divine. Why do Christians refer to the father? Because they are talking about a seed source that we came from. What about other schools of thought? What do you think?

It's hard to define this thing through a lens of fixed definitions. As the Taoists say, if we name it, we haven't really got it.

So whenever I say god, keep in mind what I've said and put aside religion or human-looking avatars. I sense that religions were simply trying to teach others about the lifeforce intelligence I am referring to through varying approaches, and I support their intentions in doing so.

* * *

One-off Power Vs Ongoing Power

Accessing the state of full connection to the source is similar to taking the popular South American plant ayahuasca. Ayahuasca awakens a large amount of lifeforce, so the consumption of it is like pumping a mega dose of Mother Nature into us.

The effect is that it activates the lower centres and purges out any toxins in the body, and also activates the higher centres in an intense way. It takes us over completely, so we are forced to surrender and give up control. This is why people experience such profound effects from it, their ability to surrender combined with the potency of its effects. It's a cocktail.

Having said that, I do not believe that psychedelics will provide the same consistent experience as naturally cultivating a self-exalted connection to our inner powers. Something just does not add up when it comes to taking the fast road on the path of liberation.

Also, the body is often not prepared for this kind of energy, so the effects can vary and sometimes be too much or may disturb the person's whole frame of existence afterward. That's why yoga puts an emphasis on a step-by-step preparation before diving into more potent practices, to ensure the person is well equipped to deal with what's happening.

I had an ayahuasca ceremony myself in the Peruvian Amazon. It was a profound experience, but it was just a one-time experience. The true transformation happened for me when I provided precise and constant attention toward myself. It's like buying a plant and taking care of it for a day but neglecting it after that.

It was probably a yogi or shaman with good intentions who started sharing the plants thousands of years ago to try and assist people in accessing higher intelligence, in a simpler way, because it helps them let go instantly.

They probably would have done some due diligence and asked them to go through a process before agreeing to allow them to partake in the ceremony. I also imagine that they would have only agreed to give it to those that were ready for it and had a deep reason to take it. Like an initiation process, or a qualification process.

These days, ceremonial herbs have become so readily available, so it encourages the shortcut mindset. I've met so many people who take psychedelics but their daily practices are mediocre. They hope for "take the drug for the super highway to peace", but don't know how to experience it without the drug.

We can't get food delivery all day long, we have to put in the work to buy and cook the foods that we want. I may sound like I am judging, but I am not. I am all for freedom, I am only trying to attempt to strengthen your empowerment muscle.

As any self-made millionaire would say, they enjoyed the ride and not the outcome. It's never about the dollar bill, it's about how empowered and equipped they feel in terms of owning and leading their life. Freedom.

In the famous hindu scripture "bhagavad gita" it speaks of not chasing the fruit, but instead performing our duties, which I'd say means focusing on the farming process.

Or we can use the cliché, "it's not about the destination, it's about the journey".

It's a very zen-like freeing way to be. I have never really cared about the achievements, I've cared about working towards getting to them, the fun and thrill of the journey. Putting my all into the art and crafting of my life, whilst being detached, playful, light and breezy.

If the journey is spent devoted to what I am doing in the moment, it's one hell of a ride because I am fully focused and mentally clear. It also means that I can relentlessly create a future, whilst not chasing the idea of it.

That's what this crown centre helps us to do, to not get so wrapped up in the game of life. To let go of the mind stuff, and fully dissolve into what's in front of us.

Letting Go and Letting In

We let life in when we surrender to the higher power outside of ourselves. We edge life out when we don't. Wayne dyer says E.G.O stands for Edging God Out.

It doesn't matter what our belief is about god, higher power, source, we can name it what we want, but there's no doubt that there is something bigger than us.

I went through a deep phase of connecting myself to the source through the path of bhakti yoga, I went to the Hari Krishna temple and added daily practices in line with this path. When I did, it opened me up to a new spectrum of energy. It fused my heart centre with the power to surrender, a delightful combo, like avocado on toast.

That is what the crown can do when it's tapped into at a more subtle level. It can infuse the power of love into a higher form of surrender. I call the heart an amplifier, a rocket fuel; it has the power to supercharge other power centres.

It helped me bring this higher form of surrender into my way of being in the world. I let go of the "self" that I thought I was and started wearing my true superhero outfit in the world.

"Becoming an image and servant of god", as they say in Christianity. Much of the Christian wisdom is powerful if you can look for the pure gold within it. They are saying to let go of the mind and let the most powerful light beam into you and out of you. They are not saying to copy some idealistic way to be, but they are saying find *your* way to be, and be it.

I am not telling anyone to believe in a religious idea of god, they can if they want. I am not saying to align to any religion. I am saying to look for the wisdom that is useful and speaks to you, rather than rules that you feel you must follow.

You know what sparks you, look for the intrinsic drivers. Look for experienced wisdom versus someone else's wisdom. Play with the exciting pulls versus a logical push.

To End

C7 puts the icing on the cake as we move toward the end of our journey because it is the path when Shiva and Shakti, yin and yang, left hand and right hand are no longer separated, they are one and they are joined through the crown to the universal one, the one of everything that exists.

All definitions lose meaning and all separation in life ends. The prayer hands sign is a practice of this communion, and so is bowing down. You see, seemingly religious practices have practical and logical purposes behind them, I started seeing that. It's why I put a red dot on my head, to try it out and see what it does, versus trying to follow a religion.

It's like when I walked onto a naked beach in Spain, something made me curious to understand what it would feel like to be naked myself. I could have pondered upon it, judged it, wondered, but instead, I got naked and tested it out. I got my answer through the experience, realising that it was pretty liberating to get naked.

So my invitation, what could happen if you let go of what you think and feel about everything?

I know for me, a whole other level of experiencing life happened.

Ultimately, if all the centres are aligned, it can lead toward the path of non-duality. And not the theory of it, I see that getting thrown around a lot after someone reads a Krishnamurti book. I am talking about actually practicing this as a way of living. Really, even naming it non-dual, means it isn't non-dual.

Perhaps I will create a new book to go into this in more depth, but I hope you can understand what I have been trying to show you in this chapter.

Take some time to reflect before you move on. I am not presenting information for you to memorise, I am simply weaving words together in an attempt to spark the part of you which wants to dance around naked and free.

We are no longer children who are looking for the "right answers" in life. Instead we can relax and let ourselves be, let ourselves explore, and be in support of whatever truth comes out from the depths of us. Not from the noise inside, but from the quiet intelligence.

✏️ Questions to consider:

What allows you to fully let go?

How do you get in the way of that? I am asking to steer you towards empowered ownership, as opposed to the common path of blaming something else or shaming ourselves.

What does it feel like in the body as an energy and experience to experience letting go? Describe it as if you were describing it to an alien.

What did you learn from this chapter? Firstly in isolation, and secondly in relation to the previous chapters.

What would you say ties us and all of existence together? Use your Einstein intuition to answer.

What are you seeking more of in life?

Final Tool-Tips

"My approach is to expose your ego so that you can see it for what it is. Therefore, I try to provoke your ego. There's nothing diplomatic about this tactic. We've been diplomatic for countless lives, always trying to avoid confrontation, never meeting our problems face to face. That's not my style. I like to meet problems head on and that's what I want you to do, too."
~ Lama Thubten Yeshe

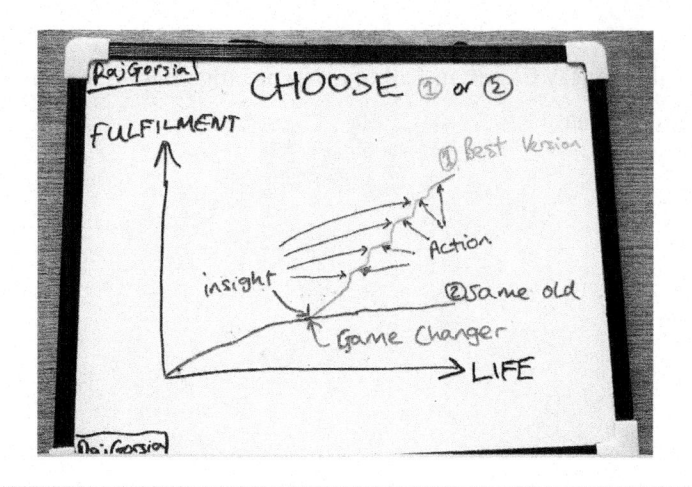

Headache to me is like over-revving a car in first gear, forgetting that I can shift gears and smooth it out. Like smoothing out cement on a wall, versus a big lump in one place.

We have these kinds of tools within us, the smoother, the hammer, the spirit level, the compass. All great tools.

My dad loves using a spirit level when he's DIY'ing. It is fascinating to watch him, he's so excited when he uses it. It helps him to build smartly, rather than building with only his mental guesses.

It's the same with our inner tools. They are exciting to use because they free us up, helping us shift gears in a smart and effortless way.

Take for example watching a performing magician. During a magic trick we are totally present, our creativity is switched on, and our sense of playfulness is activated too. How beautiful those energies are, right? We laugh when we get tricked, we use our mind consciously to try to figure out how they did the trick, and we surrender to being led by someone else, in a way that is out of our control.

I love magic, not just the theatrical acts but also being a magician in my own life. Seeing how I can creatively direct my energy, with a poise and slickness about it. Pulling rabbits out of hats.

I love the power centre system because it speaks to the logical side of me by giving me a framework, as well as the non-logical side of me to actually get into practice and test things out.

A real-life training arsenal for developing peace, bliss, enthusiasm, connection, creativity, strength, wisdom, and an expressive and liberated way of being. Everyone's looking for that kind of thing, and it's been right here all along.

* * *

Here is a summary of the power centres. Feel free to add your own associations based on any insights you've had from this book. It's more about how you understand and apply the wisdom for yourself.

These centres are yours to live with, they are a personal connection. Like having a pet, you get to know them.

There is memorising information for an exam, versus connection to the topic. Or copying someone else's homework, versus seeing their homework to ignite your own understanding. The latter is what I am here for.

Summary of Your 7 Power Centres

C1 - The Root Centre = The Grounded Physical Existence = Earth = Body

C2 - The Creative Centre = The Passion Juice = Water = Emotions

C3 - The Core Centre = The Personal Furnace = Fire = Mind

C4 - The Connection Centre = The Glue, From Me To We = Air = Intuition

C5 - The Expression Centre = The Divine Outflow = Space = Purity

C6 - The Vision Centre = The Wise Commander = Light = Synchronisation

C7 - The Crown Centre = The Surrenderer = The Undefinable = No-thingness

Practicing With The Tools

Remember this, you will develop the power of your centres by living your life full out. Working on them in a cave of solitude is an option, but I've found it really useful to use the power centres as tools for erecting a life, whilst living an everyday life. Using them with every part of the outer world, yet driven intrinsically.

Ultimately the power centres are a representation of life itself. I really want you to see beyond the mystical world and see them as tools like a knife and fork. Although I am a traditional yogi who very much talks about life being about the inner experience, I also believe that personal development takes place through outside-world actions too, by using the tools rather than just having them.

It's like having a paintbrush that doesn't paint, or a Ferrari that doesn't drive.

I know that to get better at public speaking I need to have the courage to step up and do it, and the doing of it, the speaking itself, creates more confidence and skill. So waving our swords is necessary in this life, not just having a cool sword that looks good.

There's a popular phrase that feels suitable to mention here, "Grow through what you go through". Not to use it as a dramatic past-entangling statement, but rather to embrace it as a generative, existential, and forward-moving operational term.

We regularly work out in a way that requires intense strength, and our muscles will grow over time.

We meditate for a period of time, a few times a day, and we will become more aware.

We speak in public 100 times a year, and we will get better at it.

The facts of practice. Every martial artist, dancer and race car driver will tell you that they had to get practicing for them to become better at what they do.

Here are a few examples of how the power centres can be used as tools in everyday life:

- e.g. — I am feeling a lot of pressure for a project that is coming up and I am worried about what may happen. I must use the power of surrender in the crown centre to release and connect back to the bigger picture.

- e.g. — I am unsure what to do for one part of the project, so I think and think… and think. I must become still enough to access my deeper intelligence, the intelligence that is calm and wise. I can use the grounding of the root centre to slow my body down, I can use the wisdom of the vision centre to see things differently and then access the creative centre to generate exciting ideas.

- e.g. — I want to express the reason for beginning the project to another person, but I feel stuck on what to say. I can access the wisdom of the expression centre to roar out the truth from within, rather than from my head.

- e.g. — I feel that everyone is against me and that I will be rejected when I speak in front of people. I can access the power of the connection centre to be more loving and loved by the people I am with, and rather than focusing on me me me me, I turn it into a we. And I can also ground into the root centre so I feel stable when I speak.

e.g. — I am jaded and don't feel like doing any work, I have the ideas but no energy to start them. Some doubt and judgment also kick in. I can access the power of the core centre to move my body into action and switch into a fiery mode. Rather than trying to take action from my head, which rarely works. Have you ever played sports with your head? It helps with tactics but can get in the way of the body mechanics.

e.g. — I am lacking creativity, I am not inspired and I am analysing everything and getting stressed out. I am using my thinking in a way that is against me instead of for me. I can access the power of the creative centre to free the flow of creative juices inside me.

e.g. — I have been through a breakup and I feel all alone and fragile, so much so that I feel unsafe and I feel that I am inadequately existing, so my body is on guard. I can utilise the wisdom of the root centre to help my body realise that I am safe and that there is no danger.

Finally...

e.g. — I am out of sync and have many parts of me firing all over the place, it feels like I have a crowd of people inside me. I can access the space and freedom from the crown centre to bring all of my being into alignment and access the highest part of myself.

I used to think I had a serious problem with myself. I gave myself a label of "social anxiety", I created a limitation and I lived by it. I attached to it and my entire world became colored with that paint. No wonder I was so guarded, it's because I was guarding my own limiting belief.

What I did not know back then was that this so-called problem contained a treasure chest, waiting for me to discover it. The treasure of my voice.

* * *

Final Tool-Tips

Here's a game to play with me. Try this exercise. Breathe in and visualise energy moving from the ground up through your body and out of the top of your head. Then breathe out and visualise the energy coming down through your body and back into the ground.

Continue for 21 breath cycles. Note down what you noticed through your experience. Did you find any part of your body that felt blocked? What did your mind say to you during the experience? Did you experience any pleasant sensations? What else?

This isn't a concept, it's happening to you right now, through your own doing. Self-exalted. And you gain the results from the science experiment instantly, rather than relying on a hypothesis that you haven't tested from a famous person on YouTube.

Forget them, forget me even, and look toward yourself. That's what I am here to guide you towards.

Is the sun warm? Of course, it is, that's because you experience it as a reality rather than something that someone has told you that you need to logically conclude whether it is "right" or "wrong".

That's my final tooltip for you.

✏️ Questions to consider:

What would be possible if you were to always listen to your intuition (inner guru)?

What stops you from doing so?

What is the power centre system useful for, in your own words?

Which centres feel most useful to you, if applied to your life?

Which feel most challenging to utilise?

Part Three - Beyond The Power Centres

Learning how each centre works is important, as it allows us to drive the car with potency.

Going beyond the parts, is where we learn to drive differently...

My sketch below is what I am going to build you towards, take another look at it once you finish the book and see if it makes sense.

The Power of The Path of Lifeforce

"There is a life-force within your soul, seek that life. There is a gem in the mountain of your body, seek that mine. O traveler, if you are in search of That. Don't look outside, look inside yourself and seek That."

~ Rumi

Here's an insider's view of how this book was formed. I wrote it out over a year before I began forming it into a book.

It took me ages to begin editing it. Why? Maybe I wasn't ready to release a book on such a profound topic, maybe I thought I had more to learn before I could share. Maybe my mind was in my way, or maybe it was destiny.

I like the destiny one, I think that there are moments where we connect to what I call "divine timing". It's when things click, not by force, but by resonance. Like when a baby is due, we have an estimated date, but its actual birth date is never known. Life often moves in this way.

So over a year later, it felt right, and I said to myself, I can either wait until I develop further before I release a book, or I can go ahead right now to let it move through me, knowing that future me is only an idea in my head, and present me is also an idea, one that I can detach from, whilst being fully supportive of.

Forever letting my "self" die off, and forever being reborn.

So I started editing and adding more to the book and it almost doubled in size. It began as a short article which got richer as I edited it.

But another few months after that, I began writing a brand-new chapter, this chapter. Untouched clean white paper, it feels so good. I wrote it in a semi-trance because I had a huge realisation about the ultimate path of lifeforce and how it works as a logical movement pattern. This chapter had to be added to the book to help you really understand the movement of energy within us.

I haven't formed this into words in the past because it's only ever been a felt experience, but on this occasion, I was taken to write it down in a way that made sense. I guess it was meant to be so that I could share it with you. Here goes…

What Are We?

I started having realisations that I am not the body and not the mind; that was really clear to me and it's clear for those who are aware enough to see. The common quote you might hear is, "We are not physical beings having a spiritual experience–we are spiritual beings having a physical experience".

You can get that one, right? If you really look deeply and feel this awareness within you.

The level above that is to look at the energetic body, and to realise that we are not the energy that moves through us either. As I got deeper I began to think that I was love and that I must live from the heart, but I then came to this realisation that I am not even the heart.

The deeper spiritual teachers will agree and say yes, we are not the heart, we are not the energy, the mind or the body. They will say we are only conscious of these experiences. That we are the observer.

I got even deeper–I experienced something which was not even consciousness, not even individual, and not even connected to everything. Something beyond is pure silence, pure nothingness.

Similar to the experience of going to sleep or dying, what happens? We don't know because we are beyond consciousness. We go into the dark, pure silence.

So when this experience is had whilst being awake and alive, it is so mind-blowing that I cannot put it into words because words can only attempt to paint an experience. Let's just say a few seconds of this will replenish your body and free you like nothing else in this world can bring; no spa retreat, no drug, no nothing. It is total release, total space, and total freedom.

How Does This Relate To The Power Centres?

It hit me that the power centres relate to each level of potential we have inside of us, a way of being. Like wearing a suit which upgrades as we move through them.

So to be totally free is to be beyond the experience of the power centres, and that is where the lifeforce energy wants to go.

When I say the energy is climbing, it is going towards its destined path. It's made to be born, and to die, just like we are. It has a purpose, and that is to create a penetration and unlocking of certain abilities within us and then it can rest in peace. Like penetrating a water balloon, then the water can come out freely, it's liberated.

The lifeforce's purpose is to switch on our superpowers like a lighter to a candle. Once the lights are on you can put the lighter out. The lighter's purpose is met, and it can rest easy knowing that it's done its job.

So a quick recap

- C1 represents the physical body
- C2 represents the inner network of energy
- C3 represents the mind and its will
- C4 represents connection
- C5 represents an expression of energy
- C6 represents in-sight
- C7 represents surrendering

Therefore, when I say to go beyond body, energy, mind, heart and everything else, I am talking about leveling up and leveling out the Shakti energy flow so that we tap into the experience of seeing what we are beyond these superpowers, beyond the centres, and beyond the light even.

The source energy comes in from the earth into us and the earth gets it from the sun, moon, universe, and the ultimate source. So we work as a transmitter. Therefore, to let the energy move upwards is to realise that we are beyond the experience of energy in a given centre.

And to do that we must really see the purpose of the energy in relation to each centre, so this equates to understanding that:

- the body is taking in and self-containing the source energy
- the inner network moves the source energy around the body
- the mind comprehends and uses the source energy
- the heart is a connector of the source energy to source energy outside of the self-container
- the throat expresses the source energy back outwardly
- the third eye sees the source energy and gives it focus
- the crown connects the source energy to its source again

Therefore, what I am getting at is pointing you towards being a watcher of this natural happening within us. The energy comes into the physical frame and is then being used like a machine, in cooperation with our power centres. We are really a conduit and there is a cycle moving through us; in breath, out breath, energy in and energy out, like a human circuit.

Most of the time it can be a messy output because we are not consciously using these systems inside of us. That is the whole point of having a deep-rooted awareness and an ability to act in a poised manner.

Often the sheer awareness alone helps free me from any confusion that my mind has created within me. The mind will turn the energy against me and comprehend doom scenarios. When I just remind myself of what is occurring, I can be free, instantly.

I can step back into the highest seat, the one where I am neither the stories, the sensations, the emotions, nor anything else that I think I am. I am back to being what I really am–lifeforce that comes from nothingness and is destined to be used toward a path that ends in nothingness again. Isn't that delightful?

It's like lighting a fire, there is a process of fire being created and then being used to cook something perhaps. Once you use it for that purpose, you are done with it and it can be laid to rest to go back into ash. There is no more need for fire, until next time.

That is how to use the lifeforce energy, to use it in alignment for the purposes that the power centres are made for. When we are done with it, the energy can switch off rather than linger and unconsciously make a mess, as it can very easily do. Like a fire that is left unattended, it can burn a whole forest down, especially when the mind thinks there is a problem that isn't really there.

The words I write here hit me hard because they freed me from focusing on any one centre and any one "perceived problem" because I see that I am beyond the centres, I am a conduit of a circular flow, both in the moment and as an overall life destiny.

I don't know about you, but this frees me and also empowers me to be fearless. I feel both lighter and lit up inside. The soul is in the driving seat.

All of this stuff that I think I am, they are just estimates really. I have gotten closer to the truth by means of deductions more than anything, like peeling a layer of an onion. The more I free myself with "I am not", the calmer and more composed I become.

It's a declaration to myself to let go of the attachments that my mind desperately wants to cling to. It can be scary at first, but only ever to the mind. Deep down it's an eternal gateway into forever freedom.

The intellectual mind may be tempted with questions such as, "Is this what enlightenment feels like?" But those questions are a product of the mind; "yes" is illusion, "no" is illusion. Just asking the question would suggest I am not free, and answering the question definitely suggests so. Does a person laughing ask if they are laughing? No, they just laugh. As the Buddhists say, just tree, just sit. No need to add layers.

Only the mind in the mode of desperation wishes to measure and to know. Without the answers or questions, there is freedom. Maybe that's what enlightenment is. But I will never need to know.

Let me know what comes up for you as we finish reading this chapter.

✏️ Questions to consider:

What gets in the way of your energy moving through this path of living and then dying? You can call this, energy efficiency.

What helps you to be lighter and lit up inside?

Which one of the power centres do you find difficult to connect to?

Which one connects with you most deeply?

Which questions do you often ask yourself?

The Power of Spacial Awareness - The Left And Right Wings Of The Heart

"Geometry is the harmonizing principle in nature. There is geometry in the humming of the strings, there is music in the spacing of the spheres."
~ Pythagoras

Here's another "bonus chapter" that I added. I am on a train from Athens to Meteora right now in Greece, editing the book. As I finished the previous chapter, I thought it would be useful to add a new chapter, on the topic of geometrical intelligence.

Let me start by expanding on what I told you before, the left and right sides of us have different functions, so it may feel like they are fighting at times.

Indecision or feeling pumped up, but the body is not playing ball and is saying something else. Feeling out of alignment and disoriented. You know those feelings? I faced them throughout my life.

The thing I discovered was that the left and right sides don't work well together as separate entities, they work well when they are unified. That's how it seems to work. The way to join them, as I said before, is through the heart. It's the central headquarters, it's like one of those connector plugs.

It's like a central government or a central bank. When joining ourselves and coming from the heart we move like we have wings, why else is the red bull advert so appealing? If one wing is not flowing in sync with the other wing, a bird wouldn't fly very well.

Above and below and right and left, are the dimensions of our being. I would need another book to talk about what I've discovered on these things, but for now let me give you a summary of the geometrical power that we have available to us, through physics, but beyond physics theory, and through wisdom-based usefulness.

I love usefulness, I don't need to go into the depths of the scientific formulas and get a PhD, but you can if you want.

A simple exercise to try right now to get in touch with your geometrical space is to bring your vision to a single point in front of you, and then be aware of the right side, left side, above and below.

See if you can stretch what you are seeing, this is called peripheral vision. Keep doing it for 3 minutes, don't move your eyeballs, only expand your awareness. Eyeballs fixed in the point in front, but aware of every corner of your vision.

How did that go? What did you experience? Often, people will feel a sense of calm and clarity, a waking up, and an alertness. That's what awareness is–attention being pointed, so it can create alertness, but in a calm way rather than fight or flight which usually feels uncomfortable.

Now try this, close your eyes and become aware of the dimensions of left, right, above and below once again. But this time be aware of behind you and in front of you too.

Spend 5 minutes just being aware of all of these dimensions. Then as you get familiar with it, try to stretch your level of reach. What I mean by that is that you might be aware of the space around your room to start with. See if you can stretch to your entire home, your town, your city, your country, the world, and beyond... Keep going as far as you can reach.

Remember, all dimensions: front, back, left, right, above, and below.

How did it go? What came up for you?

This is what I mean by experience versus intellect. There is no right or wrong way to do it, there is just an experience, one we can learn from. We can get so used to judging and measuring things up to see if they meet some kind of standard, that we overthink things.

This is not our voice, it's our collected beliefs of how things "should be", let's put all of that aside. We aren't in school, and we aren't going to get in trouble or be rewarded by our parents for our behavior.

That's why I love inner practices, there is no black belt, no trophy, and there is nothing we can show the world or get good behavior marks for. It's us who decides to be in the highest inner state, not anyone else.

Anyway, why did I put this chapter in here? To help you to see that you have space and that you are at the centre of every dimension. There is that term, "think you are the centre of the universe". It's often referred to in relation to egoic behaviors, people showing off or trying to impress others.

Well in the inner world, being at the centre of the universe is useful, because it's true. It loses its ego function when we say that every single human is at the centre of the universe too, not just us. It becomes universal, not personal. Now it's useful, and it's freeing, and it's connective.

A yogic quote says that the universe is the size of a mustard seed, and it's within us.

If you really feel into that, can you feel any truth? I know I can, and even if it isn't true (who knows what's true), then is it useful to practice this centring? Like brushing my teeth is useful, I don't need to believe it, but it feels useful, so I do it.

Our dimensions are multi-layered, and the more we try to speak about it and add extra mental layers to it, we go far away from the truth. That's what it's been like for me, searching for enlightenment and the answers, the code. If I tense myself with thinking, I am not relaxed enough to see the truth, through an inner experience, rather than mental thinking.

So come back to the purpose of this chapter for me, experience the dimensions. Left and right. The moment I can expand my awareness of the space around me, my wingspan is wider.

If my wingspan is wider, I have bigger wings to fly with. Not just bigger though, but also stronger and lighter wings, so now flying is a breeze.

Left and right sides are our wings. If I practice this on the train right now, I can feel a space bigger than my body, bigger than the train, bigger than the whole of Greece itself. And wow that is so darn beautiful. As an experience, it makes me smile, my smile becomes wider too, as my space becomes wider.

Imagine having all the space and reach in the world. That's what I want you to play with as I end this chapter. Huge wings, huge reach, and seeing that the entire existence is within your reach, starting from the centre of your chest.

Don't just read these words, feel these words, and experience them for yourself. Who the hell am I to say what is right or wrong? I am only saying things like a musician playing an instrument, so you can experience the waves and move however your lifeforce wants to move.

I love you.

✏️ Questions to consider:

How much space do you feel you have on an average day?

What if you had more space, what would be possible?

Can you notice a difference when trying the exercises that I laid out in this chapter?

How far do you think your awareness can reach?

Is there more?

The Power of The Duos - "As Above, So Below"

"All things, even ourselves, are made of fine-grained, enormously strongly interacting plus and minus parts, all neatly balanced out."
~ Richard P. Feynman

"As above and so below", this is a statement that I learned through hermetic teachings and it has turned into one of the most important operation principles that I have ever encountered.

It also connects to what I have been speaking about in this book about Shiva and Shakti being two parts of one whole. You can also relate it to the Taoist (and now fashionable) yin and yang symbol.

This principle of duals is a fundamental part of every religion in some way or another. Look at the crucifix, it has a point above and a point below. There is symmetry, for one side there is another.

The left and right-side work as a wingspan of the heart, they too have their own function.

I can go into depths of the practical functionality of our geometry and polarities in a whole new book but for now, I will point my words toward the purpose of this book.

Let's try to really see that each part of life has two sides to it that make up the whole. This is not to say either is bad, it's to say that they balance each other out and one exists because the other exists.

I have noticed within myself that if the centre point is not established and connected to then the two parts usually run wild. Why? Because they think they are two separate parts, rather than one.

Like a magnet, it has north and south poles, but they come from the same source.

Let's start with a few simple examples to make this real rather than theory:

Example 1:

If you throw a ball into the sky then it will move at the velocity at which it is thrown, but eventually, the force of movement will be balanced out by a counter force and the ball will come to be still again.

Example 2

Let's say you are tense and your whole body is so hot that your face goes red and your body starts to sweat (this one I felt through most of my life).

The sweat is your body's effort to create a counter-reaction of cooling inside you so that it can come back to a harmonious state of being where your body and mind can function at its most optimum.

Once the tension settles down you may begin to feel tired at some point. Again, the tiredness is counter to the high energy you had earlier. I've noticed this happen a lot when I have overworked and later faced crashes.

It's A Partnership

Everything has a recovery stroke, where the dynamic aliveness dies. The energy rises, and the energy falls. As I said before, the energy wants to live its fullest potential, and then die, and then come back again.

I am not aligned with any one belief system (I like to utilise it all) but I get why reincarnation could be true because the breath follows a similar process, constantly. Coming in, then going, then doing it all over again.

Beyond a theory, or a belief to align to, what if life was about following what made the most sense based on our lived experience?

Swimming was a huge challenge for me, I only learned how to swim at the age of 27, and even then it was just a baby step.

At the time of writing this book, I find swimming scary, but I still do it. I even pushed myself to cliff dive in Croatia, and I successfully swam myself back to shore. It might not feel like a big deal for most people, but for me it was.

All of my challenges occurred because I was not allowing the natural flow of energy to occur and I was not letting the balance occur. I was avoiding danger and pushing myself away from life, and I was adding a mental narrative to everything. A self-fulfilling prophecy was being lived.

Life has been hard when I have mentally put too much pressure and story around action or no action. Because I've attached to aliveness or attached to nothingness. Chasing both.

Chasing a win or feeling like a loser. Boom bust cycles and getting frustrated through it all. When I began seeing the natural cycle of in and out in everything and more importantly, living in harmony with it, wow everything began to change.

Life felt like a flow because I was not making everything such a big deal and I began to cherish the bumpiness of the ride.

The rollercoaster happens only ever to the mind and body, the watcher in between doesn't see it that way, the watcher is still.

Only the mind determines what something is, the thing beyond the mind doesn't, it loves and watches the ride, laughing along the way, like watching a movie and then walking out of the movie theater.

So, the true meaning of yin and yang is not in their separation of them, it's in the dance of their counteracting that makes them so powerful, together.

It's not seeing one side as good and the other as bad, it's seeing them as partners. Like roots and branches.

Eventually, I began to see that this grand power of polarities is contained within the centres too, they have counterparts.

Notice that there are 7 centres, 6 are symmetrical pairs and the heart is in the middle, it alone is a pair without having another, left and right sides to the heart (which I will explain below).

Now I will show you how your utilisation of the centres can go to another level. Think of it like having two superpowers joining forces from the top and from the bottom.

Double trouble, or should I say double strength, like those sore throat tablets which give you dual power at once, they give you both relief and energy. We get double the benefits.

* * *

So, remember the ultimate duos of: As above so below, Shiva and Shakti, yin and yang, roots and branches of a tree.

Those are the grand marriages of duos, now I will take you into duos in the context of your power centres.

Again, look for your own felt sense of wisdom rather than breezing through these words and seeing them as absolute truth.

This isn't a fact-hunting game. From my own experience, that way of operating is when my mind goes into scarcity mode, searching desperately to validate or invalidate itself, fight or flight switched on, in a subtle way.

Looking at art requires you to engage your creativity and notice what it brings up for you. I used to find this hard, but now I find it more enjoyable than rushing into reading the label next to the painting. I will do that too, but first I want to engage my inner genius.

See if you can tune into that inner genius as you continue reading.

Duo #1: The Rooted Crown

Let's start with C1, the root centre. Its function is to remind us of our physical existence, it is our physical existence. Think of a fish or an animal which walks on its hands and legs, they are primal and close to the ground. Their power centres are not in a vertical line, but they are closer to horizontal.

Watching our own backs is an essential part of animal nature, that's why the physical part of us will fire off and send us into fight or flight when there is either an actual or perceived threat.

Now look at the crown centre (C7) which is on the opposite side of the body. It's so far away from the root centre and its symbolism is opposite too. It represents the non-physical world, the part of our existence which is beyond the body, which is why it sits above the body. It is the part of us that allows us to let go of ourselves and drift into sleep, going to a dimension that is beyond us.

We connect back to the source that makes us more similar than different. We begin to feel safe and peaceful once that wisdom kicks in, and once the body is relaxed once again. The crocodile instinct has ceased and the jaw unclenches.

This wisdom comes from both the root and the crown centre. So that's what I call becoming a rooted crown wearer. Physically safe and non-physically connected, C1 plus C7 equals balance essentials.

Duo #2: The Passionate Watcher

The next duo begins with C2, the creative centre, the area of our bodies which can create actual life. There is a ton of energy moving through this area, you can throw a punch of rage because the energy down here gushes towards the body to signal it to move. You can make love and feel total ecstasy. It is an area of deep personal juice; notice the feeling you get when you read those words. Awkward at all?

"Noticing the juice" is the mechanism of C2 joining forces with C6, the vision centre. Have you ever been to the viewing level of an airport? You can watch the planes charging up and taking off, it's exciting to experience.

The vision centre has the ability to see beyond the senses, so it could feel like a confusing partnership to team up with the creative centre because the creative centre is sensual.

They say opposites attract in a relationship, I have known girls in the past who have thought that I was too cool and relaxed, they loved that about me and sometimes they didn't.

Funnily enough, in the past I have been attracted to very passionate and emotion-driven women, and they taught me a lot about feeling into life. I both liked it about them and didn't at times. That's the beauty of opposites.

Bringing these two opposites together is wonderful because it is like having the eyes to see clearly and having the aliveness to feel. What a great team that can make.

Think of taking an exam in a pressured classroom with one hour to complete it. There has to be stillness to be able to see the task from a wiser bird's eye view, as well as having the fluid for sparking your brain towards completing the exam. These two centres are like becoming the questioner and the answerer at the same time.

They are both a representation of personal potential, both seeing and feeling it.

The other centres are great supporters and assisting powers in the process, like a team. Teams work best with the right people being used for the right purposes, everyone in their zones of genius.

Team power centres is the best team you will ever hire.

Duo #3: The Solar Roarer

The sun's power is immense, isn't it? When it hits you, it hits you strongly. I grew up in London so I fondly remember the cold winter days when there would be a glimmer of sunlight peeking through onto the ground. Standing in that area was a vast contrast to the shaded area because the sun not only warmed my body up, but it also cleared my mind.

Vitamin D isn't something that comes from a tablet in a factory, it comes from the sun. The sun roars out an endless amount of supply of power to us, to all of life, it is relentless in its giving.

That is exactly what the core centre gives us too, a solar power. It distributes strength to the entire body. The only time I have ever injured myself weightlifting has been when I did not engage my core.

The core works with the expression centre in such a beautiful way, here's how my experience was and still is.

Every time I feel passionate words come out of my mouth it is like a cannon of light leaving me from below me. People ask me how I speak so rhythmically, it's because I am not using my intellect to dictate what I "should" say. Rather, I am letting a natural and beautiful volcano erupt out through my mouth.

You will see it happen with people who are furiously arguing with each other, their core is on fire, and they are spewing out venom like a snake. Wishing to inflict burns on the other through the fire inside of them coming out through their voice.

I am not saying that shouting or venom makes us failures as humans, sometimes it's a process of release. I am pointing you toward the nature of what is occurring within us, the thing that I noticed within me every time I became angry at someone. It was pure fire being switched on; dragon mode activated.

The expression centre is an energy output device, like a musical instrument. I've noticed that if there is a mess going on inside then my output will be messier. Speaking or acting becomes harder for me because the output tool isn't functioning at its best.

The core centre represents the personal furnace and the mind. Its highest purpose is empowerment, so it can either create greatness or it can create a mess.

Think of it like this, C3 holds the ability to powerfully output the fuel, and C5 represents the outflow of the fuel into purified actions, speech, and other forms of expression.

When these two centres connect to the heart, magic happens. But if the heart is not open then the two centres have the potential to make a mess together.

Duo #4: The Heart Of Two Halves

Finally, and by perfect symmetry, the heart lives in the middle. It does not have another centre that it pairs to because all the other pairs are taken. But it isn't lonely because it in itself is a pair. If you've ever taken a basic biology class then you will know that there are two sides to the heart. As I mentioned, we have two sides to our entire being.

The left side of the heart gives fresh blood to the body and the right side calls the blood back in. There is a circular motion happening during the process of in-breath and out-breath. They are partners, and they need each other to be whole. You cannot have one without the other.

And what is different about this duo is that they are physically located so close to one another, they are literally hugging in unity. They are united and they love one another deeply.

It is the perfect way to end the journey of the power centres, to see that the teaching of unity, oneness, and cooperation is happening because our entire being sees the heart leading by example in the way it cooperates with itself.

* * *

If you practice breathing through one nostril at a time, a popular yogic practice called "alternate nostril breathing", you will notice a balance of the two energies and feel replenished and perhaps a sense of bliss.

The left and right sides are connected to the power centre locations like two sides of a railroad track. The spine itself is a railroad, an energetic runway type of railroad.

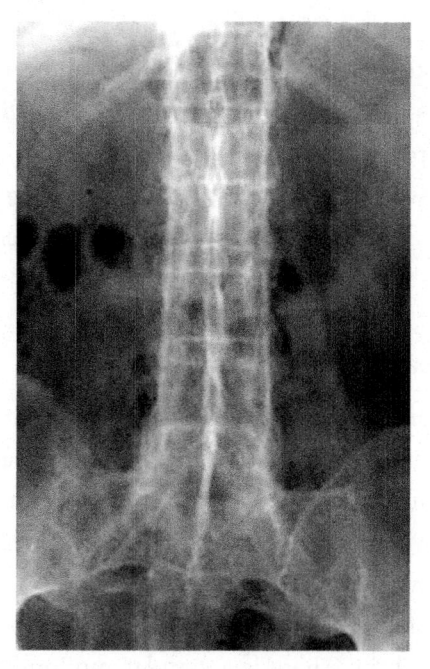

So it makes sense that the spine would contain power centres which have their own flight duty, like the different staff members it takes for a plane to fly.

The heart is at the centre of all the action, it's in the cockpit. It allows us to expand and utilise the other power centres in a more potent and sharper way because it acts as an amplifier, making everything better.

Doesn't it? Let me ask you. Think about it for a moment, when your energy has been buzzing, hasn't the same scene in life felt so different?

As I said, the heart is also a duo within itself, learn the duo of the heart and you can start expanding out to the duos of the other centres and the duos of life itself as a whole. This is what I call being a true energy master, someone who can really drive the science of aliveness within themselves.

The Duos Of Divinity

Why do you think there are so many gods in the Indian religion? I don't know what the literature says or what the head of religion would say, but through my own insights it seems like the gods represent various superpowers that we have within us.

They start with the most powerful forms of god which are all encompassing, and then they split into other gods which represent things like strength and love. Do you see why I think they represent superpowers? These gods seem to be pointing us towards modalities of operation that are available to us.

You will also see that the male gods have female counterparts, which is what I am pointing to in this chapter–the duos.

Remember, your heart, your eyes, your legs, they all have counterparts on the other side of them which they work with. This intelligent symmetry applies across so many areas of life.

So if you can really notice this, and embody the duos, you will begin to experience what ultimate harmony really means. A lovely mix of sweet and sour makes for a tasty dish, right?

* * *

As we end this chapter, remember the intelligence inside your duos and see how you can be sensitive to them during your day. Go beyond the cute and satisfying feeling that the theory gives you, and really feel into how it applies or can be applied to your life.

✏️ Questions to consider:

If you really pay attention, which of the duos mentioned can you experience? Beyond logical understanding or "I don't know".

Which duos do you see playing out in life for humans as a whole?

Which duos do you think you'd like to experience more?

How will you test out what you've learnt? It can be as simple as speaking from your core when you speak to the next person, just as a personal trainer would suggest you do when you lift weights. That's the certified PT in me speaking to you.

The Power of Power Stacking

"In art, and in the higher ranges of science, there is a feeling of harmony which underlies all endeavor. There is no true greatness in art or science without that sense of harmony."
~ Albert Einstein

There's one thing I wanted to add, which didn't feel right to tag at the end of the last chapter. It's like having a beautiful goodbye moment at the end of a beautiful phone call, and then the person says "….by the way…." and the conversation doesn't end.

So to start fresh, in every moment, "zen like", let me add to the previous chapter and tell you about the term that I made up called, "power stacking".

"Power-stacking", like the modern and trendy term "skill-stacking" is a very powerful ability to turn an avocado and a slice of bread, into an avocado sandwich. Or like mixing confident speaking with a grounded presence. Now that's a smooth operator.

Power centres are like skills, if you really think about it. Speaking is a skill, and so is calmness. But power centres go way beyond the surface level, as I've said.

They are the source of every skill. So when I mentioned the duos in the previous chapter, the duos are one stack, let's call them a symbiotic stack. Like a bicep and a tricep. A pairing of partners, a symmetrical beauty.

But like working out legs with shoulders in the gym, you can also stack any combination of centres together. Two, three, five or all seven.

All seven is the ultimate alignment, because it turns into supreme oneness, like stacking your sandwich fillings up in a perfect combination of flavors and complimentary tastes, with the right amount of sauce and the perfectly toasted bun.

Nevertheless, you can have this alignment if you work with two centres, like the symbiotic duos of the previous chapter, as well as any other combo.

The name of the game is parts working together, so it can be two parts working as one, three, four, etc. They don't need to be in any particular order either. Yes, symmetry exists between the duos, and yes connection exists with the centres near each other, but they all have a relationship with each other too.

They are like the cells in our body, relating to and with each other. Power centres are headquarter-like systems that act as a parent system to the smaller cells and functions in our body.

Just as we would be taught the different biological systems, organ systems, and bone systems in a science class. The centres are just like that, systems, but I would suggest they are higher in the hierarchy because they drive all of those systems, as well as more subtle dimensions too.

It's like speaking to the highest manager in a company, versus speaking to the staff that work below them. The change-makers are the ones we want to work with, and the highest impact occurs at the power centre level.

I've had people talk to me about their various nutrition plans, mindset techniques, or any other things they are doing to work on themselves. Often, I will see that people are working with surface-level techniques rather than going to the high-level managers.

As the Buddha said, go to the root of all suffering, and as I will say, go to the roof of all human greatness. That lies within the more subtle systems in the body.

So when I say power stack, an example could be that you wish to speak confidently about what you do. The root (C1) can be a great centre that you've worked with, therefore it becomes a powerful "skill" that you can channel. If you couple it (power stack it) with space in your expression centre (C5), you will release a calm delivery of your voice.

However, if you are working on your core centre (C3), and it's strengthened, with a healthy body you can now level up the stack, so that your calm delivery becomes a stronger delivery.

If you want to further enhance the stack because you notice that your passion isn't coming through, you can work on opening up your heart (C4) and connecting more with the audience, therefore your speaking will now be more connective and magnetic.

Perhaps you then notice that you could refine your overall centredness to tap more into your intuition to be present and in flow. Now the vision centre (C6) can be engaged and added to the stack.

You might not need to use all centres for every situation, but in some situations, you will notice that recruiting all or various power centres HQ workers will greatly enhance the output of your delivery and the quality of your behaviours.

The point I want to make is that these things become a team that you can consciously use based on specific situations. There have been times when I have been able to see things in my head and I've felt the passion running through me, but I have struggled to speak. So it reminds me to bring attention towards developing my expression centre and creative centre.

We can even use the centres as a personal development measurement tool–I've used them in that way. Assessing each to see how my development is going. It's like having a body scan machine that shows areas that are green, amber, and red. They provide an indication of what can be worked on.

Once they are worked on in a holistic way, then the stacking mechanism can be more effective. It becomes a game, one which I love to do because it makes my personal development more enjoyable as well as focused. Who doesn't love a game?

In essence, alignment of all power centres will clear the pathway for a freeing inner life and freedom in outer experience, so it's important to notice your individual development levels or perhaps we can say competence and challenges in each area.

I will end the chapter there. I hope that gave you a brief summary into a slightly more advanced possibility of the application of these centres.

✏️ **Questions to consider:**

Which powers would you find most useful to stack together and why? List some functions and examples that you can envision. Get creative, have fun with this one.

_____
_____
_____
_____

Which power centres might you find most difficult to stack together?

_____
_____
_____
_____

What does being fully aligned mean to you?

_____
_____
_____
_____

What areas of your life could do with some more alignment?

_____
_____
_____
_____

The Third Force - The Power of Living In One Symmetry

*"Wisdom is knowing I am nothing, Love is knowing I am everything,
and between the two my life moves."*
~ Nisargadatta Maharaj

The ida and the pingala, the yin and the yang, the left and the right. Mastering them both is a key aspect of life as I have said in the previous chapter. I even have a picture on my wall as a reminder of the beautiful forces of life that I have within me and outside of me.

Google definition of 'symmetrical': "arranged in a way that is balanced and harmonious."

We are made of the still power of Shiva and the dynamic power of Shakti, but remember the whole journey that I described in the book is to show you towards the natural human desire of uniting them.

Lifeforce power (Shakti) moves through the left and right channels of the body, but when it enters the central channel of the spine, which is referred to in yogic texts as the sushuma, things start to really explode.

The third eye is referred to as the third eye because it is neither the left or right eye, it is something else altogether. It is not even the combination of the two eyes as separate parts, it's not the combination of the left and right sides of our brains, bodies, and energy. It's something else…

That is what the sushuma connects to. It's the central channel and it holds the potential for every part of us to become aligned toward a new mode of being, which I have named, "The Third Force".

* * *

Unifying The Paint

If you mix yellow and blue paint, it no longer looks like yellow or blue anymore, it's something else altogether. But even this example is not even the perfect metaphor when it comes to the third force.

Why? Because the third force is something so powerful that it does not fall under the limitations of the body or mind, it's beyond the body and mind. We can say that is the divine moving through us. The bodiless power.

Throughout this book, I have been talking about the duo of forces moving through the body and how they can help or hinder us. In this chapter, I am directly pointing you toward the third force because you have hopefully now accumulated wisdom from the other chapters, or to be put in a simpler way, you are primed. So it's time for the final bomb to be dropped.

This third force, when fully expressed throughout our being is something that throws all the rules out. Once the third force is created through the centres, the centres no longer need to be focused on because their jobs are done, as they have been used as channels to move through. Entering into this third force is entering into a power centre-less state.

Third force is the oneness that I have been speaking about, which is when duality ends completely. So this is not about balancing a scale anymore, once you balance the scale and access the third force, the scale is no longer required and you unlock a new tool all-together.

Balancing is like entering a code for a padlock, once you've opened it, you don't need the padlock anymore. Third force is no longer even measured by yin or yang, it's something that cannot be measured. It's the next stage.

I used to watch Dragonball Z when I was younger, and there was this person called Freiza who evolved into multiple forms, over and over again. Until he entered into his "final form", which was a lighter, smaller and sharper version of him, with all of the powers from the previous forms intact.

It's kind of like this when we enter into the third force. The force isn't as fiery, it's cooler, but it's still potent, and it's still sharp. More so actually.

I will not go too deep into this state of being in this book, but just know that I am building on what I have said in the previous chapters (even if it may feel similar) in saying that this is the ultimate path. When the duality ends, when the power centres end and when every idea about what is what, ends.

I started noticing this when I got into deep states of meditation through the action of inner alchemy. Once the potion has been made, and drank, there can be a silence.

I could see that I could stay silent, let go and dissolve all efforts completely. All of the personal involvement ceases and I can be taken by the ocean through its natural current, whilst still being aware of my existence.

I was shocked. I spent all of this time putting in effort, only to realise that zero effort is the final path. Or perhaps better said - "effortless effort". I stopped caring as much about things that fired me up in the past, I stopped getting excited by the psychological level of stimulation such as sex, physical foods, quick buzzes, and other outside experiences.

I was experiencing everything from a different mode, one of letting go of everything, but being able to experience everything fully. All of this was experienced outside the realms of psychological disturbance, instead of from presence and observation, like a gust of wind that moves your hair.

You will see so many people in this world consumed by their political beliefs, moral beliefs, ethics, and they act aggressively to prove themselves right. They have a strong opinion and their passion is showing. In yogic wisdom we call this type of energy "rajasic", it's fiery.

There's nothing wrong with this, it's required in life. I am all for passionate self-expression, as you know. But there's a possibility for a more effective way of communicating, one that burns less energy than necessary.

When you enter into the third force, you go beyond mentally concluded morals, ethics and right or wrong. You are just there with what is, and everything is peacefully driven. It's beyond bliss even, it's the level above bliss.

Buddha and the Zen movement from Japan speak of this way of existing. It's when everything becomes contained into a state of ultimate tranquility, one that cannot be rocked. Buddha called it the middle way.

But again, before you rush off and make any assumptions about what I said and go and google it, this isn't Buddhism, this isn't Zen, this is something beyond classification in a fixed way.

I say that to slow down your intellectual brain, and to keep you engaged in the experiential wisdom inside you, not on the "right answer" in school, as per the "facts" and the scriptures, or "because that person said so" syndrome.

If the yin and yang symbol removed the split down the middle and became just a circle then you'd see what I am talking about. A perpetual state of grounding, the Japanese Enso symbol relates to what I am saying. It keeps on going; it's perfection, it's tantalising.

Try this exercise, draw a circle over and over and over and over, and see how it begins to feel.

And then do the same with your body by standing up. Spin in a circle for a few seconds and try to maintain elegance with your arms out wide in a T shape. Keep spinning until you experience an insight in relation to what I've said in this book so far.

Beyond Limitation Or Definition

This third force is powerful beyond limitation. It is calm, but it is also fierce. It's relentless actually. It's fearless and active in life, whilst being just as still as a seated meditation.

How can a person feel hurt when they do not separate the outer and inner worlds, or better yet when they do not have any separation within themselves? And when the word or idea of separation stops making sense completely?

The more times I saw myself as more or less than anyone, or tried to prove myself through my life, the more I suffered. You know, it might feel nice to criticise someone else or to judge, but it's only us who suffer.

I was beating myself up and beating others too in a subtle way. It was all because I was operating out of a limited way of seeing the world, through the personal lens of self-preservation.

Me me me me me as I talk about in the heart chapter. Even if you think you are compassionate, check how deep you've taken this; I bet there's more, I know there was and likely still is for me.

Duality and separation, instead of unity. The more I traveled, the more I realised that no matter what someone's age, language, or nationality is, there's way more we had in common than we were different.

As an exercise, try this with anyone you know. Make a list of ways you are the same and different. Really go deep into your heart when you ask yourself this, don't do it from a mind level of analysis, do it from the wisdom deep inside your heart.

Then try it with the whole heart of humanity and see what you feel after doing this exercise.

Samadhi - "a Sanskrit word that means "total self-collectedness, equanimity" Sama means same, meaning all separation ceases, and everything becomes one of the same.

* * *

The Power Of Play and Exploration

There are all sorts of conspiracies about the third eye, kundalini, enlightenment and everything else. From my experience, I cannot say I am enlightened, because how can I know? What does it even mean?

Only a mental calculation would seek yes and no questions to answer. In coding we call it the Boolean effect, yes and no being the only options, black and white. If there is a world that doesn't play by yes and no, and fixed labels, what is possible?

What if we didn't need a trophy, an achievement, or validation when it comes to this life? What if we didn't need to "get to" some honorable place where we can wow others when they see us? Seriously, see what it would be like if you took all of that social and psychological stuff away.

I don't know what word's fixed meanings are, I just use them to try to attempt to explain the things that cannot really be explained. When words stick and have a final conclusion, there is no room for shifting. This to me is stuck, fixed. I'd rather leave some wiggle room in my jeans, so I can walk with freedom in my body.

I don't need to be theoretical to walk through life, I need to understand the experiences I am having, and learn, moment by moment. If someone asks me about theory, I will give them theory, but it does not mean they will be able to experience what they desire.

If they open themselves up to experiencing, through reading these words, through watching and living life, through insight (inner sight) then they will understand for themselves rather than trusting an answer that someone else said as a fixed truth.

This whole topic of aliveness and wisdom is one of great intimacy; like a mango being eaten, the juice is tasty if we can eat it ourselves rather than someone else telling us how good it is.

I write all these words in this way to keep sparking that explorer in you, the one that knows illogically and intimately, without anyone's approval of what is right and wrong. I won't even give you that, because who am I to have that power over your wisdom?

Rather I say go for what is light and strong, not right and wrong. See, I can be playful in this whole exploration, the inner smile is like a secret handshake that lets the light in. Let's smile together.

I often make people smile and tell stories when I speak because it cuts the tense analysis both in me and the listener, bringing us back to an embodied exploration.

Neuroscientists will say that playfulness and relaxation is the state in which we are most able to develop ourselves. The door opens and we can elevate beyond our primitive system because the guard system is loosened up. I imagine a bouncer letting me into a party.

Can you feel that playfulness in you?

Can you smile for a moment?

Can you let me in?

Can you let yourself in?

Finally

The symmetry of the power centres follows the spine. There is one spine, there is one third eye, there is one sushuma central pathway, there is one kundalini shakti, there is one journey, there is one below and there is one above, there is one left and one right, and there is one centre for each area.

And throughout all of that, there is only one, one system that encompasses all of that together as one. One unified power centre. One.

Experiencing *and* embodying that during everyday life is what I call the third force. A force like no other, powerful and limitless. See if you can notice it inside of you right now, it's sitting there dancing. It's sharp, and so fearless.

The question is, can you consciously embody it, or will it run wild, hide, or never be recognised, like a diamond inside a mine. Beautiful, strong, clear, and patient. That is you. The one you.

It's closer than you "think"...

And that is where the inner journey as well as our journey throughout this book can start to naturally come to an end.

✏️ Questions to consider:

What does the third force feel like to you?

What feels like it's in the way of you fully embracing what I am inviting you into?

What would life be like if everything was one?

What was your takeaway or inner sight from this chapter?

What else would you like to explore?

What are you like when you are symmetrically one?

Conclusion - The Power Of "Living Life" Unified

"Karma simply means we have created the blueprint for our lives. It means we are the makers of our own fate. When we say "This is my karma," we are actually saying "I am responsible for my life."
~ Sadhguru

The ending of anything is bittersweet sometimes, isn't it? But when I see that life just works this way, like the sun coming up and down, then I can see that an end marks a beginning.

If we go by the cyclical nature of life, there is no end, there is only a spark of creation that floods in new insight and new possibilities.

Therefore, I will summarise the book for you in a short but sweet way that will help you continue your explorations as a traveler of life. You see, I have spent a lot of my life traveling the physical globe, and amongst all of it was always the same me sitting there as a witness to it all.

The same me who was watching and becoming wiser with every bus journey, every flight, every new culture, and every conversation. The same me whose centres were sparked by the time I lost my passport (in a scary way), sparked by the time I saw Machu Pichu and by the time I fell in love for the first time in my life.

That is us. We are a living embodiment of these power centres; they can be sparked unconsciously by the outside world, and they can be sparked consciously by us. The whole point of this book is to show you that these centres hold the superpowers that we are born with and that you can use as teammates during this game of life.

As I say, they are happening anyway, so we may as well get to know them and use them better. Right?

Like how our stomachs digest food, our breath breathes, and the sun wakes us up. It's all happening anyway, so what if we support the efficiency of these processes by consciously being a dance partner with them?

This kind of empowered involvement can turn life into living, a noun versus a verb. Verbs are a happening, nouns are things.

Try to imagine living life without understanding what living or life truly is. It's like living life not knowing who your parents are, you would want to go on a search and discover where you came from. Something would just not feel right.

It's the same with our inner plumbing; if we know it better then we can end the eternal confusion and scarcity, come home, and find the things that we are searching for. Not only that, but we can use the things we find, for living life.

I've met searchers throughout my life, and I've been a searcher throughout my life. I searched during travel, romance, thrill experiences, food, and any other feeling of stimulation to try to feel like I was not lost.

Social media enhances this searching, the companies know this, and that's why they encourage things like reel and montage videos. It gives us a machine gun spray of dopamine. Listen to your body the next time you are scrolling social media and see what's going on inside you.

Do the same anytime you engage in any activity. Are you doing it to move toward something or to move away from something? Are you feeling calm and full, or restless and incomplete? Asking myself that question has changed the way I engage with life.

In truth, the only thing that has given me a true feeling of peace and empowerment is cultivating autonomy over my inner workings, and then using that power, out in the world. Rather than hunting for things on the outside to give me an inside power.

It's like swimming against a tidal wave, it wouldn't feel good because the flow doesn't work that way. The best surfers know how to attune themselves to natural intelligence, inside and out. That's what the centres are: intelligence, headquarters, powers, bridges.

Here's a quick recap of their powers:

- C1 - Physical Grounding
- C2 - Creative Juice
- C3 - Inner Strength
- C4 - Connection Mastery
- C5 - Fearless Expression
- C6 - Inner Sight
- C7 - Letting Go and Letting In

At this point in the book you must have some ideas of how to work with these powers for yourself, and at this point in the book you may be wishing to know more about stepping down this path of life mastery.

Now I can give you some more direct guidance because you may be interested in it after moving through this book.

I run live experiential programs, meaning together we drive through these centres systematically so that you can really transform and use them with more precision. See my website (www.withraj.com) for more info.

* * *

The Living Kind Of Life

The power centres are like a train track. I have tried my best to demystify the train journey and to teach you about the path in a way that is not too "woo-woo" or extreme right-wing spiritual (as I like to say).

I have gone beyond the fluff and theory and given you the truths based on my experience with life. My wisdom will continue to expand, so I can revisit if anything needs updating.

Remember this, the power centres are like outfits that you can wear. I know some people who will literally use the color coding of their centres to choose what they will wear on a given day. You can either call this silly or call it smart.

Conclusion - The Power Of "Living Life" Unified

Either way, if it's helping a person bring greater power into their life then who's the silly one? Who's going to lose out, the one who laughs and stays skeptical, or the one who tries things out and supports their fellow human in doing the same?

I am not too into colors myself, you may catch me wearing bright colors at times but I am not consciously coordinating my outfits to centres. Instead, I tend to align myself through the inner experience of awareness of the centres.

I notice the nature of how I am reacting to things, and I then summon the superpower I need as and when I wish to reset my perspective and energy state. You may call this meditation, or perhaps we can call it "instant insight".

I can do it in the moment by checking in with my heart, stomach or third eye; it's a living meditation, a quick shift of gears. You can do this too, try it. If you don't get it straight away that's fine, I developed this skill over the years, a lifetime of having a noisy and harsh critic inside me made it a little harder.

Remember that practicing the art of awareness and practicing using your superpowers is key. This isn't a theory; it has to be a living embodiment of who we are. Like having a sword, it can either hurt us or it can help us cut through trees in a forest.

It's wonderful that we have these personal mastery tools available to us. We just have to use them, not theorize or get a spiritual or intellectual ego about them. Tools are to be used. Imagine being a lumberjack who studies trees but doesn't cut them, he'd be a fraud.

A lumberjack isn't a lumberjack if he doesn't cut trees, and humans aren't humans if we don't really live. That's the thing I realised after being stuck in a maze inside my head for most of my life. I wasn't trapped because of the thinking; I was trapped because I wasn't living in the world. I was living in my head.

A prison that was disguised in righteousness and safety, with nobody to talk to but myself. That's what they use to punish prisoners, put them into a room with nobody. We do that to ourselves; it's normal but it also isn't natural. We weren't designed to be trapped in our heads, we were designed to explore and be a lifeforce.

I call it dead living when I get into my head, I call it living deadly when I am out. I made a YouTube video about this if you want to see, the essence is that I am beyond all fears when I am living deadly, and when I am dead living, it feels like my life is a greyscale photo.

We Are Specially Designed

The five elements, the power centres, the yin and yang, amongst many other fundamental laws of life govern us. We cannot exist without the sun and moon, this is a fact. The same with our power centres, we require them to live. Therefore, imagine what's possible if we can unlock the highest extent of their abilities.

Someone once said to me, Raj you are operating at 10%, imagine you dialed that up to 20%? What would be possible? I didn't know it at the time because I did not have the wisdom of 20%, but when I did, I was amazed. I wondered, what would 22% be like? Or what if this 20% is now my new normal, my new 10%?

In life, we go through ups and downs, so it isn't possible to always be high all the time, and I now realise that. But like a stock on the stock market, we can have downs but if we are on an upward trajectory overall with our health, our freedom, and our expression of our lives as a whole, imagine how great it will be over time.

And check this. I use the previous paragraph as a reset tool, a seed of stabilising the mind, like asana in yoga. Then I take it to the next level of wisdom by coming back to the lesson from the third force. Who says what is up and down?

It's the intellect. The ultimate truth is that there is no up and no down, there is only a different level of realisation, less smoke in the way of seeing what has been there underneath, pure ecstasy and peace, as well as ultimate creative power.

That's the ultimate unification.

Conclusion - The Power Of "Living Life" Unified

So let's end this book with a prayer. I don't have one for you, however. Instead, I invite your intelligence in and invite you to say one for yourself. This doesn't have to be a religious prayer.

What is religion? It seems to be some people who discovered the same inner energy that I am pointing us toward. That religion is ours to learn, not to be told by someone else.

We cannot describe how to dance, the person has to just get it for themselves. It's energy meeting awareness, Shiva Shakti, yin yang, all polarities becoming one. That's why it feels good to smile, we go into our most natural way of being.

So say your prayer, do your dance, and embody your truth. It's yours. So are the power centres, get to know them like getting to know a puppy. I will guide you through a meditation track, through a talk, an event, through practices, through my own stories, and through any words I share with you.

I will give you frameworks, tools, and ways of accessing your treasures, that's my job. But remember, my words aren't to be repeated like a parrot; find the truth and then speak words that seem like they serve you best.

They may be the same as my words, if you really feel them then they become yours, like passing on a tradition or a recipe, and then adding your essence to it. You make it your own.

I love what I am passionate about so much that I don't look for praise for my words, I am happy to be low in levels of IQ. I don't want to sound intellectual or scholarly, and I don't wish to create scholars or intellectuals in this world.

I am not even a writer, I am only spilling words out onto a paper to see if can spark something in you, to spark the you in you.

I wish to create greater life experiencers, energy masters, action takers, and light-bringers. Free, fully expressed and happy humans who really know themselves and know life. That to me is meaningful.

That's the wisdom of these 7 power centres and the wisdom of life. That's the lifeforce that wants to move through me and through you.

Write to me if you wish to have some guidance in exploring further. I have some pathways that I can direct you towards. Through this book, through my online resources and programs too. Check my website (www.withraj.com) to find out more details.

*　*　*

Being A Guide

I am so happy to be doing the work that my grandfather set me out to do– to be like him, a trusted guide. He came to me during meditation experiences over and over again, I kept asking if it was real and he kept saying yes. It felt so real, I was with him.

Over months and months, we kept meeting, and he kept helping me to learn, to let go of my old self, to awaken, to bring lifeforce into my life and finally to lead me towards the path of sharing the intelligence of this lifeforce with the world.

He told me, not through words but through visions and intuitive whispers. I had an insight that I am meant to be the latest of Indian leaders in this modern world. It felt so right and so aligned. A gush of honor moved through me, like watching my nephew perform on stage. I guess that's the child in me, happy for me.

The exciting part is that I know that I present the ancient wisdom differently because I have a British Indian man's perspective.

I did not grow up in India, I was born in London, so I know the Western mindset. However, I have realised that I am well equipped to keep the blood going and sharing everything that is coming through me from my ancestors with the modern world.

A holistic consultant for the modern age, but still an ancient yogi at heart. I like to say that I feel the blood of a thousand yogis running through my veins. It feels so natural and easy, it's in my genes. I love what I get to do, with my granddad inside me and beside me. I wear his chain and I summon him whenever I am in need.

Conclusion - The Power Of "Living Life" Unified

He insisted on calling me Raj-esh. My mum didn't want that name but he insisted; he knew what I was made for whether it was consciously or unconsciously. Something transmitted the name to him.

Raj means king, Rajesh means lord of kings. I translate that to "freer of human greatness", or "leading leaders".

My middle name is Bharat, it means illuminating fire, it's also the precolonised and Sanskrit name of India. Bharat has powerful meaning, and I represent it proudly.

I love you for listening and being with me on this journey. This book isn't about me, my grandfather, or even about power centres–it is about you. So keep working on being more of you. The super-powered you.

You have it all, I have it all, we have it all. It's primed, our only job is to move all obstructions out of the way and to embody what we intuitively know inside, outside into the world.

Like switching gears in a car, we can switch on each power centre whenever we want, if we know which switch does what.

When all the lights are on and aligned, the third force explodes a bliss through us and dissolves us into the nothingness that we came from, like an ecstasy that isn't so short-lived and times a million.

After the freedom of nothingness, I notice that I am left with everythingness. A mode of operation that has unbelievable levels of calm, aliveness, and fearlessness.

If that isn't living into our true potential, then I don't know what is.

Unity, becoming unified, being united on all fronts. And then going and living this darn life, full throttle and full stillness. That's what makes life a living to me.

Never forget it, never stop exploring, and always stay true to yourself.

As Ramana Maharishi said: "The journey of life is a journey of self-discovery. Explore your true self, and you will find the answers to all your questions"

Enjoy your journey. I am with you.
Raj

✏ Questions to consider:

What did you get from this book as a whole? One big insight that has changed the way you see the world.

What is one action you will commit to embodying as a result of reading this book?

Which power centres can you relate to the most, and which less so?

Conclusion - The Power Of "Living Life" Unified

What do you want to learn more about in relation to this book?

Do you know how to drive from these power centres?

What would you love me to share more with the world through the spirit of my grandfather?

About the Author

Raj Gorsia is spearheading a new era of personal development through his unique approach known as "lifeforce." Central to his vision is "the school of lifeforce," an ethos and methodology harnessing energy for personal growth.

Raj engages individuals through personalized coaching, group leadership, workshops, and speaking engagements. His voice serves as his superpower, inviting readers to immerse themselves in his audio experiences, which convey the passion and wisdom he seeks to impart.

In the contemporary landscape of personal growth, spirituality intertwines with science. Raj, a British-born Indian, embodies this fusion, drawing from both modern scientific principles and ancient Eastern practices. With a background as an ex-Big 4 consultant, he offers a distinctive perspective shaped by his experiences.

He proudly stands among the forefront of leaders in this domain, often asserting himself as "the best in the world at this." However, he invites scrutiny devoid of ego. Explore his body of work, engage in dialogue with him, and ascertain the truth of his claim firsthand.

For further details about his programs and mission, visit www.withraj.com.

Printed in Great Britain
by Amazon